PRAISE F

The Survival Guide
to British Columbia

"When I first met Ian Ferguson I called him an arrogant easterner—he did live in Alberta, after all. But since moving to BC, Ian has discovered all our embarrassing secrets. This is the essential guide to Canada's wild west coast."

MARK LEIREN-YOUNG

winner of the Leacock Medal for Humour for *Never Shoot a Stampede Queen* and author of *Real Magic Secrets Revealed*

"He's like a brother to me."

WILL FERGUSON

author of *Beauty Tips from Moose Jaw*

"One-third practical, one-third odd, one-third enlightening, and one-third bloody hilarious.* If a provincial guide and a stand-up comedy routine mated, this book would be their bastard love child. Worth getting arrested for. Please send bail."

CASSIE STOCKS

winner of the Leacock Medal for Humour for *Dance, Gladys, Dance*

* based on Ian Ferguson's arithmetic skills.
(Thank God he writes better than he maths.)

"Also, he's very funny. You should buy this book."

WILL FERGUSON (again)

"Somewhere in Kamloops is a hipster Welsh fashion designer who is going to be about as happy with this book as she is with her Canucks season tickets. But that's okay, because any one of the rest of us who have lived in or visited BC is going to get one of those ice-cream-headache/hernia-kind of injuries from laughing at Ian Ferguson's latest address to the nation."

J. MARSHALL CRAIG
author of *Eh Mail* and *Megalife: The Autobiography of Nick Menza*

"As a lifelong Torontonian, I'm not sure why I was asked to review this particular book. I wondered if no BC writer would agree to read it, let alone wax poetic about it. However, having finished Ian Ferguson's very instructive and fact-filled treatise, I now feel prepared for anything BC can throw at me. On a more serious note, and believe me, nothing about this book is serious, my sides are still aching from reading this special guide. Line after line, page after page, Ian Ferguson keeps the laughs and satirical insights coming. Clearly he's bucking for a second Leacock Medal. And this may well win it!"

TERRY FALLIS
two-time winner of the Leacock Medal for Humour

"Some people think of British Columbia as nothing more than a place to film movies for tax breaks, or a convenient spot to put the business end of a pipeline. Ian Ferguson, however, understands that there's more to us than that—we're also brimming with deadly wildlife. And this survival guide is deadly funny."

CHARLES DEMERS
author of *Property Values* and the Juno Award–nominated *Fatherland*

"Sure, the British Columbia Tourism Association won't speak highly of Ian Ferguson ... but he will live on in my heart as a very entertaining writer. (He may not live on for much longer, mind you, as the province is due to try to kill him again. Pick up this book while you can still get him to sign it!)"

ALI HASSAN

stand-up comic, actor, and host of CBC's *Laugh Out Loud*

"In the past, Ian Ferguson has seen fit to tackle the big subjects. He has square danced with topics like how to be Canadian and what's going through the mind of Justin Trudeau, both large, amorphous subjects. This time he's set his aim a little smaller, specifically taking on Canada's westernmost province. Laced with Ferguson's trademark wit and observant style, *The Survival Guide to British Columbia* is a book that will educate those from different hemispheres about the province's benefits and problems, and amuse those more local who are aware that British Columbia is neither British (anymore) nor Columbian (ever). You will learn about the importance of salmon to B.C. residents (excluding vegans), and oddly enough, how the Welsh are viewed. You should be prepared to have your perception of that noble land forever altered. I laughed. I cried. I longed for a Nanaimo bar. It's that tasty."

DREW HAYDEN TAYLOR

award-winning playwright, filmmaker, and author of *Chasing Painted Horses* and *Take Us to Your Chief: and Other Stories*

THE SURVIVAL GUIDE TO BRITISH COLUMBIA

IAN FERGUSON

HERITAGE

VICTORIA VANCOUVER CALGARY

Heritage House Publishing Company Ltd.
heritagehouse.ca

Cataloguing information available from Library and Archives Canada

978-1-77203-284-0 (pbk)
978-1-77203-285-7 (epub)

Edited by Lesley Cameron
Proofread by Marial Shea
Cover and interior design by Jacqui Thomas
Cover and interior illustrations by Jacqui Thomas

The interior of this book was produced on 100% post-consumer recycled paper, processed
chlorine free, and printed with vegetable based inks.

Heritage House gratefully acknowledges that the land on which we live and work is
within the traditional territories of the Lkwungen (Esquimalt and Songhees), Malahat,
Pacheedaht, Scia'new, T'Sou-ke, and W̱SÁNEĆ (Pauquachin, Tsartlip, Tsawout,
Tseycum) Peoples.

We acknowledge the financial support of the Government of Canada through the
Canada Book Fund (CBF) and the Canada Council for the Arts, and the Province of British
Columbia through the British Columbia Arts Council and the Book Publishing Tax Credit.

23 22 21 20 19 1 2 3 4 5

Printed in Canada

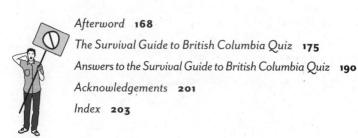

Foreword

I **once wrote a** newspaper column in which I said Ian Ferguson looks like a photocopier repairman.

It was meant as a compliment. There's no authorly affectation to Ian. No turtleneck sweater. No hipster skinny jeans. No too-cool black leather jacket. No haughty disdain. Instead, I wrote, he could blend into any Tim Hortons in the land. Good for him.

Therefore, I was shocked—shocked, I say!—to read the following line in this book: "British Columbia is the worst-dressed province in Canada."

Et tu, Ian? Is this how you act after we British Columbians welcomed you into our comfortably disheveled midst? Is this how you slip in the knife even as we embrace you like one of our beloved old-growth conifers?

Yes, yes it is—and that's a good thing. Let me explain. First, when Ian says we are worst-dressed, that is not necessarily a bad thing (if preening like a peacock were important to us, we would flash our feathers, not wear moth-eaten Fly United T-shirts to work, grad ceremonies, the opera, or when officiating at weddings). Second, he doesn't so much stick a shiv in British Columbian ribs as tickle them. Ian is one of the wittiest, funniest people I know, and who doesn't like funny?

And third, we all need friends to tell us the truths to which we are blind when we stand too close to the trees (or hug them; see conifers, above) to make out the forest.

This is Ian's great gift: recognizing absurdities in the things that others take for granted. Stephen Leacock called this "the kindly contemplation of the incongruities of life." Those incongruities are the heart of satire, which is a particularly Canadian kind of funny.

Satire is an outsider's form of humour, one that comes from standing back and looking at things from afar, from taking in the view from high in the bleachers, where it's easier to see that down on the field, all is not as it should be. It's no accident that Canadian satire's greatest practitioners tend to come from the edges of the country: Eric Nicol, a three-time winner of the Leacock Medal for Humour, hailed from one of Canada's bookends, British Columbia, while Rick Mercer and the 22 *Minutes* crew emerged from another, Newfoundland. Note that *Saturday Night Live*, that pillar of 'Merican parody, was created by another outsider, Canada's Lorne Michaels.

This pattern extends to Ian, who grew up in a place that is as far from mainstream Canada, geographically and in every other way, as Trump is from Trudeau. Fort Vermilion, Alberta, a tiny flyspeck on the sprawling pink map of the Dominion, was where he wound up after his dad piled the family into their 1953 Mercury Zephyr and drove north from Edmonton—way north, not far from the Northwest Territories. How and why they came to live there, six kids in a no-running-water, no-electricity cabin, is a ripping yarn, entertainingly told in *Village of the Small Houses*, the memoir-of-sorts that earned Ian his own Leacock medal in 2004. (And let me pause here to argue that *Village* should be required reading in every high school in the land, so accurate is its description of life in a certain slice of Canada at a certain point in history.)

Urbanites might be surprised to learn how the Ferguson kids fared once they left what was described as the third poorest community in Canada. Ian became a bestselling and award-winning author, playwright, actor, and director. Brother Sean gained note (as it were) as a composer and professor at McGill University. Brother Will also became a bestselling author and Leacock winner.

Imagine that, two Leacock laureates in one family. And that's not even mentioning the Leacock nomination Ian and Will earned for the humour book they wrote together, the gazillion-selling (not that I'm jealous, much) *How to Be a Canadian (Even If You Already Are One)*. That book also won the 2002 Libris Award for non-fiction. I'm pretty sure that makes the Ferguson boys the Canadian Arts scene's version of hockey's Sutter brothers.

If Torontonians are stunned that this sort of success should have been enjoyed by someone from, well, anywhere but Toronto, others will argue Ian's unconventional background is what allowed him to see Canada in a different light. "I really did feel like, when I left Fort Vermilion, I had come to a foreign country," he once told me.

He might say the same of moving to British Columbia, as he did a few years ago. And not just any part of the province either, but Vancouver Island, which is like BC squared. If BC marches to a different drummer, the Island dances to a horn section that no one else can hear at all. To plagiarize myself: it's where the rest of the Great White North shovels its flakes.

The thing is, for such famously free-spirited people, we British Columbians tend to get awfully uptight when people poke fun at our loopiness (or, frankly, at anything else). As you will discover by reading *The Survival Guide to British Columbia*, taking offence (particularly on behalf of others) is one of our favourite hobbies.

Or perhaps, if you recognize yourself in that description, you might just want to give this book a miss. Frankly, if you are so fragile or humourless that you cannot take a little affectionate-but-accurate joshing, if your default setting is Self-Righteous Indignation, or if your reaction to the phrase "trigger warning" is not an eye-rolling smirk, then you should probably spare yourself the grief. Trust me, you will melt, little snowflake, you will melt.

On the other hand, if you have enough confidence to laugh at yourself, you'll enjoy the read. And if you actually are a baffled newcomer trying to navigate life on the right side of the Rockies (that's "right" as in "better"), you'll find it essential.

—Jack Knox

Jack Knox is an award-winning columnist for the *Times-Colonist* newspaper in Victoria, BC. His is also the author of three bestselling books, including *Hard Knox: Musings from the Edge of Canada* and *Opportunity Knox: Twenty Years for Award-Losing Humour Writing*, both nominated for the Stephen Leacock Medal for Humour.

Introduction

So you've arrived in British Columbia. Good for you. You may be just passing through, although where you'd be passing through to, considering the location, is a question for another time and perhaps another book. Your options are limited. You may be planning to stick around for a while or even make the province your new home. Perhaps you're just visiting and consider yourself a tourist or traveller. Welcome. Please leave nothing behind but footprints and money. Perhaps you've enrolled in one of BC's fine post-secondary institutions of higher learning—or possibly one of the many private colleges or trade schools, some of which are actually quite reputable. Again, thank you for your contribution to the economy, and here's hoping your diploma in hair extension technology pays off. You could even be—fingers crossed—a skilled tradesperson, in which case, geez, thanks for stopping by, we could really use your help. Any idea when the drywall will be delivered?

No matter what has brought you to the westernmost part of Canada, you should be prepared for what awaits you. The place is pretty, from top to bottom, but also pretty scary. If you're coming to BC—for whatever reason and for however long—you should be aware that a lot of what you're going to deal with will ... how's the best way to put this? Kill you. BC will try to kill you, sometimes with kindness, but still.

You'll need to be ready to cope with disasters, both natural and unnatural. On the natural side there will be forest fires, floods, blizzards, heat waves, avalanches, mudslides, rivers running red with blood, plagues of locusts ... Something for everybody, really. BC's department of tourism recently changed its advertising slogan from "Beautiful British Columbia" to "BC: Come and watch the biblical prophecies unfold."

On the unnatural side, you've got gas prices, raw sewage pumped directly into the Georgia Strait (as well as the body of water bearing the same name), disarticulated human feet washing ashore, unvaccinated children coughing their lungs out, what passes for the Vancouver Canucks penalty kill, politics in general (and municipal politics in particular), and bicycle lanes ... Endless, endless bike lanes.

These will all try to kill you, except for the Vancouver Canucks penalty kill, which (despite the name) will just break your heart. I know what you're thinking. "Bike lanes? Seriously, how will bike lanes try to kill me?" And, "How dangerous could a local mayor actually be?" Oh, just wait. Or, skip to Chapter Two or Chapter Seven. I don't mind if you read ahead. You paid for the book, after all. Unless you're the type of person who likes to read the first few pages of a book before deciding to purchase it and you're currently standing in a bookstore attempting to arrive at that decision, in which case let me just point out that I still get my royalties, whether you pay for the book or not. As long as it leaves the store, I get paid. So, I'm not counselling you to shoplift, because, uh, that would be really, really wrong and probably illegal. I'm just saying that if money's a little tight, don't worry about my end.

Where was I? Oh, right. Even if you can find a way to avoid catastrophes, you will still have to make your way through BC and deal with British Columbians and British Columbianisms. For your own safety and security, you should learn the customs and culture of BC in order to avoid mishaps or misunderstandings.

Now I can hear you ask another question, the most obvious question really, which is probably something like "What qualifies you to write a survival guide to British Columbia?" or "Why should I listen to your advice?" or "Do you think those are real security cameras in this bookstore?" Something along those lines, and I certainly don't want to put words in your mouth. It's bad enough that I can hear you.

Here's the thing. I am a survivor of British Columbia. The province tried to kill me the first three times I visited. Let me explain. When I was in grade two, my family took a road trip from my home town in northern Alberta to BC. My mother originally hails from Burnaby, so I believe it was some sort of family reunion. We did visit our big-city, or at least large-town, relatives in, I think, Abbotsford and Ladysmith. It was the middle of the summer, blisteringly hot, and the car overheated on our way up the Mount Robson Pass. We pulled over to both let the engine cool down and stretch our legs, and I got distracted by some sheep, or possibly goats, as they tiptoed up an impossibly sheer cliff. Defying both the laws of gravity and common sense, and to get a closer look, I leaned so far over the tubular steel safety railing that I fell. Fortunately, a passerby had been paying attention and was able to grab me by my ankles and, with a little help from other concerned bystanders, hoist me to safety.

My next encounter came when, after cleverly deciding to drop out of high school to explore the rewarding and challenging field of manual labour, I ended up working on a seismic crew outside the fabled metropolis of Atlin, BC, located just south of Teslin, which is in the Yukon, or just Yukon, the "the" having been dispensed with long ago. Hope that helps. Not that you'll ever go. I took it upon myself to fix the propane tank that was supposed to heat our water so we could shower. I used a lit match to illuminate the nether regions under the hot water tank. I had also left the gas valve open. It didn't go well.

My third time wasn't the charm. Altitude was once again my downfall. I decided to drive from Vancouver to Calgary during a heavy rainfall. During the winter. Apparently rain turns into snow at higher elevations.[1] You may already know that. And not dry Prairie snow like I was used to, but thick, moist mountain snow. The higher I got, the steeper the road, and the slower I drove until the car started sliding backwards. I white-knuckled it to the Coquihalla toll booth before turning tail and heading back south. By the time I made it to the parking lot of the A&W in Hope, the snow had turned back into rain, and I relaxed just enough to drive into a culvert.

So those are my bona fides. My first three visits to British Columbia and the province tried to kill me all three times. I nearly plummeted to my death, was almost burned alive, and just about careened to my doom. This created an initial impression of BC as a place where your life is constantly in danger. And yet I survived.

Why blame BC? Why not? Sure, these incidents were, technically, my fault and an indication that I don't have the common sense that the good lord gave to garden mulch, but this sort of thing doesn't happen to me anywhere but British Columbia. For example, I had my first ever car crash in BC. Got rear-ended in Langford on Happy Valley Road, which wasn't nearly as much fun as the name would imply. I have lived, worked, and driven in Edmonton, Toronto, and Los Angeles and never had a traffic accident, not for lack of

---

1   Heavy rain turns into heavy snow, or "a blizzard" in the vernacular.

trying but because the provinces of Alberta and Ontario and the golden state of California don't want to kill me.

I blame the scenery here. It's a distraction. Keeps drivers from concentrating on the road and paying attention to what they're doing. Or maybe everybody really is stoned.[2]

It's not just the traffic. Everything in British Columbia is dangerous. The location, the people, the politics, the culture, the activities, the fashion, the climate, the "job" "opportunities,"[3] even the recreational choices ... You risk your safety and security just by setting foot in BC. Take it from me. I've made mistakes and learned hard lessons the wrong way and wrong lessons the hard way. I've had to adapt. I've gained wisdom. And I want to pass this knowledge on to you so you don't suffer the same trials and tribulations that I have. You'll suffer different trials and tribulations.

What you need is a well-researched, clearly written, and comprehensive guide to surviving and thriving in Canada's most westerly province. This isn't it.

However, the information contained in this book will allow you to experience British Columbia with minimal damage to your health and well-being. Remember, BC *will* try to kill you.

All statistics contained in this book were accurate at time of publication or completely made up for comedic effect.

No guarantee or warranty is offered or implied regarding the advice or recommendations offered, and you follow any or all of the instructions at your own risk.

Despite all of the above, I confess to now making my home in Victoria, because weather.

9

---

2   Here's a helpful hint: Marijuana is legal, it's not compulsory.
3   This ever-present danger creates the kind of stress that can lead to wildly excessive quotation mark usage.

MAP OF BRITISH COLUMBIA

1
- loggers
- miners
- Chinese buffets
- actual winter

2
- farmers
- vintners
- some tourists
- lots of snow

3
- city slickers
- urbanites
- recent arrivals
- lots of rain

4
- fishermen
- retired rock stars
- lots of tourists
- overcast with sunny breaks

5
- politicians
- septuagenarians
- tons of tourists
- sunny with periods of rain

6
- mountain climbers
- campers
- refugees fleeing Alberta
- dystopian weather and politics

1 Location, Location, Location

SURVIVING YOUR ARRIVAL

To prepare myself for the task of writing the definite (and possibly definitive) survival guide to the province of British Columbia, I embarked upon an extensive and thorough period of research and analysis. Which is to say, I stopped by a bookstore and thumbed through a couple of travel guides just to see what, if any, inspiration I could glean and if there was something useful I could adapt for my own purposes. It's not plagiarising. It's what the kids nowadays call "sampling."

The first thing I noticed was that every travel guide (by which I mean both) I read (by which I mean glanced at) started with the obvious. They explained where the place was located and how to get there. Now this isn't a travel guide; no, sir, it's a survival guide. It's far more important to get things off to a good start when the general well-being of your reader is at stake. But those points are still a good place to begin. British Columbia: Where is it and how do you get there?

Let's begin with where it is. British Columbia is located on Canada's Pacific coast, isolated geographically (and politically and culturally) from the rest of the country. You've got the Rocky Mountains along the border with Alberta forming a natural boundary between the two provinces. You've got pipelines, existing and proposed, creating a greater (albeit metaphorical) barrier between them, and you've got hockey, which is the single greatest obstacle between Alberta and BC.[1]

On the western side of the westernmost province you've got the Pacific Ocean. Well, actually, depending on which way you're heading, first you run into the Strait of Georgia and/or Puget Sound and/or the Juan de Fuca Strait and then you bump into Vancouver Island, but once you get past that, then, yeah, you're finally at the Pacific Ocean, and it's clear sailing from then on. I want to point out that, yes, this is the exact same Pacific Ocean that warmly laps at your ankles when you're wandering the Santa Monica coastline with your shoes in one hand and a cold beverage in the other, and it is also the same Pacific Ocean that rejuvenates your spirit and your body when you're immersed in its warmth while swimming off the beach of your all-inclusive in Puerto Vallarta. It's just much, much colder up here.[2]

To the north is the border with the Northwest Territories, Yukon (or "the" Yukon) territory, and, of course, the US state of Alaska. There is a controversy associated with this last-named neighbour. When the Russians sold Alaska to the United States (for $7,200,000 and a president to be named later) in 1867, the eastern border of what is now called the Alaska Panhandle had never been settled properly. It took until 1903 to sort out the dispute over the boundary. Since Canada had just become a country in 1867, I believe everybody was too busy partying at this point to notice the Americans take a big chunk of BC as their property. The Tlingit and Haida weren't happy with this turn of events either, since they suddenly had an international border running through their traditional territory.

13

---

1   Alberta has twice as many professional NHL teams as BC does.
2   Much.

To the south is the 49th parallel and the borders of the US states of Montana, Idaho, and Washington. The US capital is also called Washington, but it doesn't border British Columbia. It doesn't come anywhere close. To avoid confusion, just remember that there's the Washington State that borders BC, and the other Washington that's in a perpetual State of Confusion. Or that Washington State lies to the south of British Columbia and the other Washington just lies. Whichever mnemonic device you prefer is fine. Oh, and just in case this isn't confusing enough, there's also another Vancouver in Washington State, just close enough to mess up MapQuest and confuse your GPS.

South of the 49th parallel it is still possible to be in BC. Most of British Columbia, just like most of Canada, snuggles up against the US border for warmth. Some residents of BC huddle below the border. The southernmost tip of Vancouver Island is actually closer to Bellingham, WA, than to Vancouver, BC. If we followed the border right across the island, everything south of Nanaimo would be in the USA. Think of it as a trade-off for the whole Alaska Panhandle debacle. I mean, when you get right down to it, which part of British Columbia would you rather have hung onto?

When North Korea launches its missiles and the United States retaliates with its anti-ballistic Strategic Defence Initiative, most of the bombs will end up falling in BC. To ensure your survival, you should arrange to be in Vancouver when this happens. In 1983, the city council of Vancouver passed a resolution declaring the municipality a "nuclear weapons free zone." They even erected signs leading into the city to let you know they had taken steps to protect their residents: "Welcome to Vancouver: a nuclear weapons free zone." When the incoming missiles are redirected, they will notice the signs, change their trajectory, and end up landing in Surrey or Richmond. Not a good day at the Brooklands Aviation Museum or a particularly lucky one at the River Rock Casino. If only the civic leaders of Surrey and Richmond and, well, every other community in BC had been as forward-thinking and progressive as Vancouver's.

Don't worry. The chances of this happening are very remote. You're much more likely to be caught in an earthquake, "the" earthquake, or The Big One, before this happens. Most of the province of BC is part of the Cascadia Subduction Zone, a rather earthquake-prone area, which includes the Leech River Fault, the Devil's Mountain Fault, and, the most volatile fault line of them all, the Juan de Fuca Plate. This may sound like something you could order off the White Spot "light lunch" menu ("I'll have the Wanda Fuca Plate, with extra cottage cheese and hold the maraschino cherry") but it is—just—slightly more detrimental to your health. Scientists warn that British Columbia is way overdue for something they call "a massive super-thrust earthquake," which isn't hyperbole. That's the actual understated scientific name. Yikes. Your best bet to survive will be to avoid any soil liquefaction hazard zones. So don't be near the Tsawwassen Ferry Terminal, or most of the Lower Mainland, or anywhere on Vancouver Island, or ... You know what? Cache Creek will probably be safe. Anything west of there will become beachfront, which would be a good slogan for a land developer: "Why go to the ocean when the ocean can come to you?"

That's the thing about BC, you have your choice of natural or man-made Armageddon. Oh, you can also worry about forest fires, but it's the resulting suffocating smoke that will be your real problem, as in "Armageddon sick of these air quality advisories." If you're genuinely concerned about burning to death, hang around Henderson Lake. It's not just the rainiest community in British Columbia; it's an actual continental (yes, as in the whole of North America) record-holder. And Metro Vancouver gets rain for almost half the year, which is why the city flower is mildew. Some good news: the threat of civil unrest is now fairly low, since the Canucks aren't likely to make the playoffs, so you can easily avoid riots.

Now that you understand where BC is located, and why that makes it dangerous, it's time to understand how to get there. You can arrive in British Columbia by land, sea, or air, or any combination of the above. Which is another reason British Columbians don't feel they have a lot in common with their neighbouring provinces: there are not a lot of cruises heading down the North Saskatchewan River, and bicycling into Winnipeg is really only advisable during the narrow six-day window between winter and black fly season.

Let's begin with Land. There's a lot of acreage in British Columbia, and much of it is accessible by motor vehicle. Although there are no proper highways, let alone an actual freeway, so don't get your hopes up.

If you drive into or around BC, you'll notice many of the twisting and turning mountain roadways have no shoulders or safety barriers or, apparently, rules. You will want to keep your eyes on the road and not pay attention to the scenic view or you will end up becoming part of the same breathtaking landscape you've just been admiring. Also, the large illuminated signs that other places use to give drivers updates on road conditions are used here for social engineering purposes. Rather than tell you about fog patches on the Malahat or a collision on the Lougheed Highway,[3] the messages will read "Don't follow too close," "Did you remember to be mindful today?" and "Eat your vegetables." So, not a lot of help, but they are right about the vegetables.

---

3 Don't let the name fool you. It's a residential road, not a proper highway, and the sign designating it as such is purely for entertainment purposes.

You will also encounter bridge congestion, which is a term you'll have to become familiar with, since the highway planning department seems to go out of its way to make sure that roads and bridges aren't compatible. It's sort of like bridges are Macintosh and the roads are Microsoft. If a bridge does happen to lend itself to traffic flow,[4] this is usually accidental and the immediate solution is to slap a bicycle lane or two on it.

Case in point: the Burrard Street Bridge in Vancouver. I lived in the Kitsilano neighbourhood for a while and used to walk across that bridge two or three times a day to an office downtown. Traffic was always moving, and there were a handful of pedestrians and bicycle commuters cheerfully sharing the sidewalks, smiling at each other and wishing each other a good day. Sometimes we sang together. It was a simpler, gentler time. Then the planning department noticed that there was one remaining bridge that wasn't gridlocked and it slapped heavy concrete barricades on either side of the bridge to create euphemistically termed "temporary" bike lanes. The result: traffic jams, frustrated drivers, and, perhaps counterintuitive to the point of the whole exercise, an increase in air pollution from all the idling internal combustion engines. Also road rage, bike rage, and pedestrian rage when everybody decided they had to take sides rather than share the roads. If you're driving outside of the city of Vancouver, you'll want to keep an eye peeled for moats,[5] more properly called roadside storm ditches. These are designed and maintained by the Ministry of Transportation and Infrastructure of British Columbia to keep out invading armies and deter dragon attacks. They are also just a ton

17

---

4 The brand spanking new Port Mann Bridge solved this problem by using falling chunks of ice as a deterrent.
5 Or chasms.

of fun when you're driving on roads without street lights. Especially if you don't know where you're going.[6]

When you drive in BC you'll also want to be wary of "pedestrian-controlled intersections," which are flashing green lights that don't change to amber, let alone red, until and unless a pedestrian pushes a button (hence the name), which is a little different from the rest of the civilized world, where a flashing green light means you can now make a safe left turn. I first encountered this while driving from my Kitsilano apartment to my office. Imagine my surprise. Now you know why I ended up walking to work. Also, you should know that drivers in British Columbia don't signal, although they will virtue signal.

You will also notice a lot of honking. Some of it will be from flocks of Canada geese (gooses? geesen? geezers?), but most of it will be from your fellow drivers. This applies to the entire province, from picturesque rural laneways to four-lane (gasp!) urban streets masquerading as highways. Only the city-state of Toronto creates more cacophony. Drivers will honk: A) to warn you, B) to shame you, C) at all other times.

While driving in residential neighbourhoods, you'll encounter "traffic calming" measures, which do anything but, and you will want to prepare yourself for traffic circles, which are a safe and efficient way to ensure traffic flow, again everywhere else in the civilized world, but which the local drivers are still getting the hang of. Many of the roundabouts are sponsored by auto body repair shops, although the ones leading into the airport in Victoria (you have to navigate three traffic circles in a row to get to YYJ) were paid for by the Chamber of Commerce in the hope that a percentage of drivers would grow tired, give up on

---

6 Fun is being used sarcastically here. It's a terrifying addition to your driving experience, right up there with encountering wildlife crossing the road.

the idea of circumnavigating their way out of town, decide to stay, and maybe open a business.

Remember though, when driving in BC you should drive like a local, so ensure that wherever you go you are impeding as much pedestrian traffic and endangering as many bicyclists as possible.

But, uh, hey, you might be the type of person who chooses to travel by bicycle. If so, you're in luck. BC has a whole series of dedicated bike lanes and protected cycling corridors that you are welcome to ignore. If you want to fit in, you'll want to ensure that wherever you cycle you're impeding as much automobile traffic and endangering as many pedestrians as possible. This is assuming you're a real bicyclist, with a helmet and cycling shorts, and a rainproof, wind-resistant Mountain Equipment Co-op official riding jacket made of genuine Super Micro Quantum fabric. Oh, and a sense of entitlement.

The other kind of cyclists, by the way, the type wearing a baseball cap and cowboy boots and sporting lip tattoos are either A) recent parolees, B) gentlemen who have just had their driver's licences taken away, or C) actually bicycle thieves.[7] You might think you should avoid them, for safety's sake, but they can be a more convenient way to arrange a bicycle than U-Cycle and, unlike the bike rental and bicycle sharing companies, they are absolutely free. All you have to do, when one of these "cyclists" (note the intentional use of ironic quotation marks) pulls up next to you smoking an unfiltered Number 7 extra-length and muttering darkly about their overdue child support payments, is shout "Hey, that's my bike!" and they will drop the bicycle and run away. Or stab you with a sharpened toothbrush.[8]

19

---

7   The answer is, more than likely, D) all of the above.
8   Or shank.

You can also come to BC via VIA. That's if you're feeling nostalgic and you have a ton of disposable income. Train travel used to be cheaper than flying but more expensive than taking the bus. It divided the country into three clearly delineated groups: rich people flew, the middle class travelled by train, and the rest of us took the bus. Those days are long gone. Speaking of the bus, if that's your preferred mode of transportation, I have some bad news. The Greyhound bus service has kind of quit operations in British Columbia, leaving a patchwork assortment of local companies to take over the more popular routes. Which is fine if you're going from one more or less major centre to another, but if you want to get from, say, Nelson to Creston (and here I would assume you lost a bet or were fulfilling some sort of parole requirement), you're going to have to trust your safety to Dougie and his 1987 Dodge Caravan.

You could also walk to BC, if you've got enough spare time. If you opt for this method of transport, remember to try and fit in. Crosswalks are to be used as a last resort. There is no need to look up from your cellphone when stepping out into an intersection. And a secured bike lane is the perfect place to stand still and check your messages. You will want to impede traffic and endanger yourself, just like a real British Columbian pedestrian. One cautionary note: If you're walking across the border with a duffle bag full of weed in some sort of coals to Newcastle tribute, be aware that your trip is unnecessary and superfluous. BC Bud may be harder to get ever since pot was legalized in Canada, but British Columbians still take tremendous pride in their locally grown product and will be resentful of what they consider to be inferior imports. Also, you will get arrested. And there's no "surviving your incarceration" chapter in this book, so I'm afraid I won't be able to help you.

Catching a taxi in BC isn't as easy as it is in other places. Hailing a cab is not just impossible, it's also illegal. You're supposed to use your phone or go to an approved Taxi Stand, which is what you'll end up doing. Standing for a long, long time waiting for a ride to come and pick you up. The number of licences issued to taxicabs is woefully inadequate in every city (population of Greater Victoria: 367,770; number of cabs on the road at any given time based on my personal experience: 12), and the province is still stalling on licensing ride-sharing companies. They aren't in a rush to let Uber set up shop (and they aren't all that keen on Airbnb either) so if someone offers you a lift, they don't mean Lyft, and you probably shouldn't get in, unless you recognize Dougie from your trip to Creston.

So, since taking a cab isn't convenient (population of Metro Vancouver: 2,463,431; number of cabs on the road at any given time based on my personal experience: 9), you may need to rely on public transit. The appropriately named BC Transit is in charge of this form of transportation and offers commuter bus service in most major cities and towns in British Columbia. And Kamloops. You can travel on a double-decker bus, a bus that is hinged in the centre (also known as an articulated lorry, but only by residents of Oak Bay and West Vancouver), or a bus that is carbon-neutral. None of them will arrive on time.

Rapid Transit is really only available in the greater Vancouver area, which boasts the SkyTrain (or, if you're a fan of *The Simpsons*, a Monorail), essentially a driverless subway car. Which is a just a tad concerning, but if you think of it as a really long horizontal elevator, you'll calm down. The weird thing about the SkyTrain system, besides nobody actually driving, is that they've only just got around to installing gates in the stations to ensure you pay your fare before

21

getting to the platform. This was done on the honour system for years, the idea being that the number of people riding for free wouldn't cost as much as adding secured entrances. Then human nature and basic mathematics came into play and you now have to actually jump a turnstile to evade paying for your trip just like in other cities.

Let's move on to Sea. The shoreline of mainland British Columbia, the shoreline of Vancouver Island, and the combined circumferences of the Gulf Islands add up to almost 10% of Canada's total coastline. This is due to the number of inlets, which are ubiquitous, as opposed to outlets, which are used to power-up your smart phone.

If you arrived in BC by water, you may have been a passenger on a cruise ship or taken the Black Ball Ferry up from the US. You will have noticed that cruise ship terminals in British Columbia resemble industrial parks. The main departure points are in Victoria, at Ogden Point, a vast oasis of concrete and aboveground parking, and Vancouver, where the billowing sails of Canada Place welcome you to the tourist-friendly neighbourhood of Gastown (soon to be renamed RenewableResourceEnergytown), which is mere steps away from the slightly less welcoming neighbourhood of East Hastings, also called the Downtown Eastside, or DTES, or, for the more classically inclined who appreciate a good Dante Alighieri reference, the 7th Circle of Hell. And yes, it is right next door to where all the cruise ship passengers disembark. Here's a helpful hint: When you step out of Vancouver's cruise ship port, walk straight ahead or turn to the left. Do not make a right turn.

The ferry from Seattle will take you to the Inner Harbour of Victoria. Once you clear customs, you'll be greeted by friendly volunteers, cheerful buskers, and overjoyed panhandlers, all of whom will be hoping you are from the United

States and here to take advantage of the very favourable exchange rate between the US dollar (in slang: "the green-back") and Canada's currency (*en français: le peso du nord*). You will also assume Victoria has a problem with the local skunk population. Not true. That's weed.

BC Ferries operates the ferry system. (The branding and marketing folks in British Columbia tend to be literalists. You got your BC Transit, BC Liquor Store, BC Hydro, BC Bud, etc.) The ferry routes are ostensibly part of the highway system, which doesn't exist, which is why you'll be walking onto (or driving aboard, I'm not here to judge) what may, at first glance, resemble a smallish cruise ship. This can be disconcerting if you've just stepped off a real cruise ship. There are gift shops for buying souvenirs, promenade decks for enjoying the view, and computer work stations for ignoring the view. You can also get food, if you're on one of the ships that offers a buffet, or "food," if you end up on one of the ships with an onboard White Spot. And for 12 bucks you can also sit in quiet contemplation in the Sea West Lounge, where children, loud conversation, and cellphones are prohibited. Best money you'll ever spend.

Most of the ferries have grandiose names like *Spirit of the Two Sailing Wait*, *Queen of No Other Options*, or *The Overpriced Princess*, which is also an obscure Hans Christian Andersen fairy tale about a cursed kingdom that is incapable of building a bridge to the mainland. If you head off the beaten path, or to put it in nautical terms, into less charted waters, the ferries will have more practical names such as *Northern Escapade*, *Big Tough Boat*, and *Island Connector*, this last so named because it is where people who work and live in rugged remote communities connect with tourists looking for adventure and authenticity. Here's a helpful hint: If you wear a brand-new flannel shirt and shiny new work boots you will be instantly and easily identified as an outsider. The locals will leave you

23

alone and you'll be able to sit in quiet contemplation without having to shell out any extra money.

The ferry system is a vital link in the transportation chain, and also a monopoly, which may explain why tickets are almost prohibitively expensive. Note that I said "almost." The management of BC Ferries are world leaders in incremental fare increases and surreptitious supplementary charges. Here's a helpful hint: To find out when the least popular day and time to travel on your preferred route is, you should pay the additional reservation fee. You'll be guaranteed a spot on a mostly empty ferry. Maybe. If you arrive too late they cancel your reservation. And if you arrive too early, they punish you by putting you in the "time-out" section of the parking lot. If you don't make a reservation, you'll quickly learn what times and days are busiest. You might as well settle in and enjoy your delay. Once you're on board, don't imagine a rejuvenating nap in your vehicle. That's not allowed. For safety reasons. And so you'll spend money. Oh, one more thing: Those electronic signs giving you the odds on making the next sailing? Less helpful than the ones on the highways.

You can also travel by water in delightful little tugboats, called water taxis, that are used by commuters and visitors alike in many of the port cities. Make sure you tip the British remittance man piloting the boat to get him to shut the hell up and let you enjoy the scenery, otherwise you'll be listening to anecdotes and opinions, both unfounded, for your entire journey and you'll wish you'd taken a regular old land taxi instead.

Let's finish up with Air. Not the kind you breathe, the kind you travel through. And not, usually, hot air, unless you're flying into the provincial capital.

There are airports in every major city in British Columbia. And Kamloops. They are mostly well appointed and all look like they kind of want to be art galleries. Every terminal in the province has sculptures, installations, and paintings both for your aesthetic enjoyment and to distract you from the confusing signage. Trying to catch a connecting flight and want a simple, easy-to-read sign that tells you where to go? Good luck with that. The same people who write the electronic "information" signs on the "highways" (one more time, all use of ironic quotation marks is intentional and deliberate) also came up with the confusing, frustrating, and essentially untranslatable demotic wording used in all the airports. Some sharp computer programmer should develop a Rosetta Stone app to make sense of it.

You can also fly on planes that land on water. To do this, you can take a seaplane or a floatplane. The difference between the two is that a floatplane is a small, fixed-wing airplane[9] with pontoons where the wheels would normally go. A seaplane is a flying boat. One takes you from Nanaimo to Vancouver for that important business meeting and the other one takes you to Haida Gwaii for that once-in-a-lifetime salmon fishing trip and then back to the closest hospital to get the Coho Killer Black Nickel rust-resistant fishing hook removed from your philtrum. Or possibly your glabella.

You may, of course, wish to combine all the possible varied and whimsical modes of transportation into one. You could, for example, drive across the Peace Arch Border Crossing, take a BC Ferry from the Horseshoe Bay Terminal to the Duke Point Ferry Landing, and then catch a flight to Kamloops. The only risk would be the boredom of the endless lineup at the border, the inertia of the three-sailing wait for the ferry, leaving your car parked in Nanaimo (it will get broken into), and, of course, Kamloops.

25

---

9   Like a Twin Otter, proudly manufactured in BC by Viking Air.

2 Talking and Arguing

SURVIVING YOUR CONVERSATIONS

When travelling to a new destination, it's important to be able to communicate with the local population. Going to Mexico? Learn a bit of Spanish. Heading off to Japan? Well, it couldn't hurt to be able to say more than *konnichiwa* and *domo arigato*. And ignore Dennis DeYoung's suggestion that you can follow up saying "thank you" in Japanese with "Mr. Roboto." The Japanese are a polite people, but even they have their limits. Suppose you decided to head off to Europe. You would want to be able to at least order a *tasse de café en français* or a *tazza di caffè in italiano*. Although you should probably cut back on the caffeine.

Even in Canada, you will want to be aware of the language differences from province to province and city to city. Taking a trip to Montreal? They speak French there. Ottawa? They speak obfuscation. In St. John's they speak a form of English, Newfoundlandese. Just getting the accent down may defeat you, but it's worth the effort if you do go. You'll probably bump into Gordon Pinsent.

This chapter will help guide you through the various regional dialects, accents, and insults used conversationally by the residents of British Columbia. You will also learn how to pronounce "Tsawwassen."

British Columbia is a bilingual province. Oh, not French and English, although many residents can argue and complain in both of Canada's two official languages. Over a quarter of the population (or 25% in metric) does not speak either English or French as their first language.

Here, in more or less descending order, are the most common languages spoken in BC other than *les deux langues officielles du Canada*:

1) Cantonese
2) Mandarin
3) Punjabi
4) German
5) Tagalog
6) Korean
7) Spanish
8) Farsi
9) Italian

I know, I know ... You're wondering why Welsh didn't make the list. Not significant enough numbers, population-wise.

There are also 30 (or two and two-fourteenth stones, in standard imperial measurement) different Indigenous languages and 60 (or 40 cubit) distinct dialects spoken by the almost 200 (or 198, to be exact) First Nations of what is now British Columbia, including Salishan, Tsimshian, Dene (including but not limited to Tlingit), Wakashan, Xaad Kil, and Kutenai/Ktunaxa.

I know, I know ... You're wondering why Cree didn't make the list. You will see Cree in BC, but they all moved here from the colder regions of Canada.

The province of British Columbia has incorporated a lot of words and place names from First Nations. Place names like

Osoyoos, and Shuswap, and, of course, Tsawwassen. And efforts are underway to include even more Indigenous language. The Queen Charlotte Islands are now called Haida Gwaii, Mount Douglas is now also called Pkols, and there is a push to rename Mount Newton, or rather return its traditional Sencoten name, Lau Welnew. This naming move is in recognition of the fact that most of the province is on unceded Aboriginal land. So this may be guilt or a true attempt at reconciliation by the non-native population, but either way, it is mighty white of them.

There's a plethora, or possibly panoply, of languages spoken in BC, but the usual means of miscommunication is English. However, despite this theoretical common language, the residents of BC do have their own unique way of speaking. Speaking of which, they often aren't on speaking terms with each other or the rest of Canada.

British Columbians do speak Canadian. You will hear "deke," and "give'r," and "pogey," just like in the rest of the country, eh? This should come as a relief. However, you will encounter some expressions and turns of phrase used only in the province. Slang, in other words. Actually, those are exactly the right words (or "right word" according to the *Canadian Press Stylebook*) to use ... Slang. Or, you know, "some unique British Columbian lexical characteristics specific to the region." Whatever.

Here then, are some helpful British Columbianisms:

- **Choked (pronounced "tʃoʊkt"):** not an emergency requiring the Heimlich Manoeuvre or an erotic request requiring the Heineken Manoeuvre, but an expression of annoyance or anger.

  Sample sentence: "You wouldn't believe what Save-On is charging for one bottle of Kombucha Wonder Drink! I'm choked!" Or, "I'm choked that capitalist economic monetarism has so influenced the fiscal policies of BC, no matter which political party ends up in power."

- **Chuck (pronounced "tʃʌk"):** from the Nootka word for "water," usually combined with the English word "salt" to create "saltchuck"—literally "salt water"— to refer to the ocean, specifically the body of water between Vancouver Island and mainland British Columbia.

  Sample sentence: "Taking a ferry across the saltchuck to a bonspiel on the mainland." Or, "My contact lenses are so dried out; I'm going to soak them in saltchuck."

- **Doeskin (pronounced "dā -skin"):** has nothing to do with Bambi's mother. It is what the locals call a plaid lumberjack coat.

  Sample sentence: "Didja get that doeskin at Mark's?" Or, "I'm choked! I just spilled kombucha on my favourite doeskin!"

- **Skookum (pronounced "skuːkəm"):** means terrific or first class. This is taken from the Chinuk Wawa word for a monster or giant.

  Sample sentence: "Hey, Drew's put together a skookum team for the bonspiel." Or, "Styx was a skookum band, but they haven't charted a hit song since the invention of the internet."

- **Skookumchuck (pronounced "skuːkəm/tʃʌk"):** take the meaning of "skookum" (robust) and add the meaning of "chuck" (water) and you get a compound word meaning "rapids." Although this expression may have become a sociolect used exclusively by white-water rafting guides and their customers.

Sample sentence: "Geez, I booked a skookum Squamish River trip and I'm gonna do the class 5 skookumchuck." Or, "It was raining so hard today, Denman Street turned all skookumchuck."

- **Squatch (pronounced "skːwɒtʃ"):** a derivation of the word "Sasquatch,"[1] this is used in BC to refer to large, hairy men—usually with poor personal hygiene.

Sample sentence: "Hey, check out the squatch tossing third rocks for Drew." Or, "Don't stand downwind of that squatch over there."

- **Kokanee (pronounced "kəknǽ"):** from the Shuswap name for salmon, it is also a well-recognized brand of beer, and is used as shorthand for any beer as long as it's cold and available to consume.

Sample sentence: "Hey, toss me a Kokanee." Or, "That's skookum Kokanee that squatch snuck into the rink in his doeskin."

In mainland British Columbia, "Back East" refers to the rest of Canada, which is to say any place on the other side of the Rocky Mountains. They call Vancouver Island "The Island," which irritates the folks on Salt Spring. On Vancouver Island the rest of Canada is referred to as "the mainland." In BC, "The Rock" isn't the name of a mildly talented action star and ex-CFL linebacker, it's how you refer to Vancouver Island if you're hip. Or hep. Also what

---

1 British Columbia's version of Big Foot or Yeti, the Sasquatch is mythological. Like a stay-at-home Canucks defenceman.

you throw at a bonspiel. Nanaimo is "Hub City," Kelowna is "Orchard City," Kamloops is "the City of Broken Dreams." I think. "PoCo" is simply the abbreviation for the city of Port Coquitlam, "Ditchmond" is a mildly derogatory term for the city of Richmond, "Slurry" is a slightly more disparaging term for the city of Surrey, and "Coastie" is an absurdly offensive term the rest of the province uses to refer to Vancouverites.

Which brings us to insults. These are geographically based. Every single part of British Columbia, from the Cariboo to the Kootenays through the Okanagan and beyond has its own unique regional identity. And a large part of that identity is defined by hating the other regions.

"But wait," I hear you ask. "When do we learn how to pronounce Tsawwassen?" Be patient.

For your safety, you have to learn which topics of conversation to avoid in which areas of the province and the subtle differences in connotation that arise due to your location.

You don't want to call an unemployed pulp mill worker from Howe Sound a "tree-hugging, latte-sipping, granola muncher," and you don't want to tell an unemployed Kerrisdale barista that they are a "tree-killing, beer-swigging, animal mutilator." This will just cause confusion, and annoyance, and possibly danger.

Canadians in general, and British Columbians in particular, are quite easily offended. "As a ___, I find that offensive" is heard more often in day-to-day conversation than "Howzit going?" and you have to be prepared. Canadians, especially British Columbians, also lead the world in being offended on behalf of others. What would be considered an innocuous comment elsewhere can quickly escalate into an argument, or even worse, a lecture.

You will want to avoid using expressions like, say, "It's all Greek to me," or "Mexican standoff," or "Pardon my French," even if you aren't talking to someone whose family originally hails from Greece, or who traces their ancestry to Mexico, or is from Quebec. Working with bright, ambitious, and slightly rebellious millennials? Don't refer to them as "Young Turks." Having lunch with a British Columbian? Offer to "split the bill," do not, under any circumstances, suggest you "go Dutch." And you are much safer, if you've been eating with your fingers—you know ... burgers or wings or such—to ask your luncheon companion to pass you a "moist towelette" than to ask for a "wet nap." If "Walk Like an Egyptian" suddenly starts playing in the mall (and here I'm assuming you'll be sharing your meal in a food court) do not, no matter what, start dancing. Although you can still "welsh" on a wager or even "welch" on a bet, since the one ethnic minority you can safely mock in British Columbia is the Welsh.

Here's a case in point. I was engaged in casual conversation with a British Columbian recently. This fellow was red of hair and pale of skin. He looked like he travelled exclusively by tunnel. It was supper time, I was feeling peckish, and he said we should grab a bite to eat. I suggested going for Chinese, which resulted in me receiving a lecture on the differences between what constituted authentic Asian cuisine versus the historical oppression and institutional bigotry behind the creation of what the average Canadian calls "Chinese food." This seemed odd to me, since I had already noticed the most popular restaurants in the entire province are Chinese buffets, but I had to put up with this homily. Again, I will point out this guy was so Caucasian he appeared translucent. But he had offered to buy.

I told this story to a friend of mine who is of Chinese heritage, and she thought the guy was being ridiculous. This was reassuring, although she didn't like me referring to him as a "ginger," since that's apparently a word only redheads are

MAZE OF OFFENCE (IN A BAR)

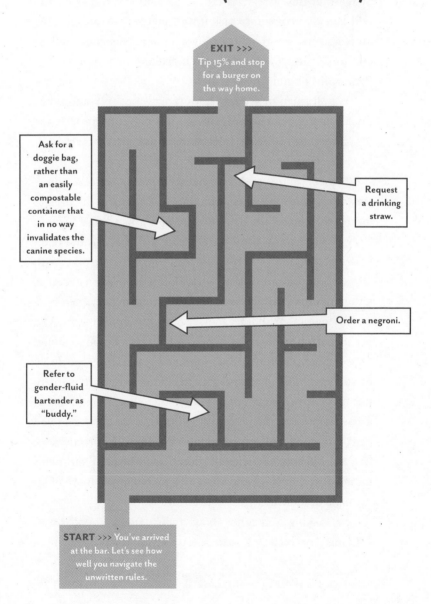

EXIT >>> Tip 15% and stop for a burger on the way home.

Ask for a doggie bag, rather than an easily compostable container that in no way invalidates the canine species.

Request a drinking straw.

Order a negroni.

Refer to gender-fluid bartender as "buddy."

START >>> You've arrived at the bar. Let's see how well you navigate the unwritten rules.

allowed to call themselves. They prefer "melanin challenged," I suppose.

British Columbians are particularly sensitive to any language that has perceived ethnic or cultural overtones and will quickly take you to task if they feel you are speaking in an insensitive manner, even if you're not. This is part of the culture of the province, and you'll just have to put up with it. Personally, I blame the Welsh.

We all learn to avoid certain topics of conversation. You don't bring up politics, religion, or money in conversation, eh? It's better to stick to safe subjects, such as sports, or family, or even the weather, right?

I've got some more bad news for you. You can, sometimes, get away with sports small talk if you take the time to learn the name of the local team. "How about those Salmon Kings?" used to be a good starter in Victoria, but the team folded in 2011 and was replaced. Now you'd have to open with "How about those Royals?" which could be misconstrued as either an attack on or a defence of the monarchy.[2] You're safe with "How about those Chiefs?" but only in Kelowna. And you could talk about the Kamloops Blazers if you've somehow ended up in Kamloops. You know, your car broke down or you were taken hostage. The BC Lions only work if you're not in Vancouver (where nobody cares about the CFL) but anywhere else in the province (where they do care), and you can't go wrong complaining about the Canucks penalty kill. But you will run into British Columbians who consider sports to be not so much entertainment or recreation as more of an example of the violently toxic patriarchy.

So, asking someone about their family, then? Nope. Although this is considered safe territory pretty well anywhere

34

2 "Royals beat Prince George" is the sort of sports headline that Fleet Street might misconstrue. Especially if the Royals won in a shootout.

else, in British Columbia it's fraught with peril. The person you are chatting with may take umbrage at what they consider too personal a subject or, worse, if you ask them about their family they may tell you about them. In other places, "How's the family?" is usually answered with "They're fine," or "Braden is off to summer film camp," or "They grow up so fast." In BC, such banalities (and truisms, kids really do grow up fast) are often replaced with far too much information about the complicated and often difficult relationship the person you are talking to has with their spouse/children/parents/partner, and/or ex-spouse which will be explained, expounded, and even espoused far past any interest you may try to feign.

How about the weather then? Well, in the rest of Canada, this is the go-to as far as initiating a dialogue, and it's usually phrased as a question. "Hot enough for you?" "Is it cold enough for you?" "Wet enough?"[3] Like that. In British Columbia, although you will have to survive weather (and Chapter Five of this very book will provide you with many helpful hints for how to do so), you should not talk about the weather. It's sort of the equivalent of fight club. Here's why:

"Hot enough for you?"

"It's only going to get hotter unless we do something immediately to halt climate change!"

Or:

"Hey, is it cold enough for you?"

"Yeah, I wish that global warming would hurry up and get here!"

And:

"Wet enough for you?"

"Of course it's wet! We live in a rainforest! Why wouldn't you expect it to be wet?"

35

---

3 This according to Margaret Atwood, as quoted by my brother Will in the introduction to *How to Be a Canadian*.

Even:

"Nice weather, isn't it?"

"Not if you have to sleep outside on the street!"

These aren't conversations you want to have as a new-comer to the province. So, what's safe? You certainly don't want to discuss gas prices. That's a whole different kettle of fish, or "pipeline of remonstration," as they say locally. Well, when in Rome, do as the Romans do. Just don't ever use the expression "when in Rome, do as the Romans do." Pay attention to how British Columbians do things. At some point in your travels, you'll be asked by a local person what brought you to British Columbia. This is the British Columbianism for "Where are you from?" Now asking somebody where they hail from is a perfectly fine question anywhere else in the world, but in BC this would be considered a microaggression. What if the person is from Kamloops? Who would want to admit to that?

When asked "What brought you here?" it's perfectly accept-able to say "A boat" or "An airplane" or "A car," as long as you pay attention to your surroundings. If you're in Vancouver or Victoria or surrounding areas, you'll probably want to modify "a car" and say "a hybrid" or "plug-in electric net-zero personal vehicle." You know what? Skip the car thing entirely if you're in Kitsilano or Fernwood; just answer "A bike."

This will probably not entirely satisfy the person asking you the question. There is also a slim chance that they will understand you were making a small joke. Hypothetically you could have this conversation with a British Columbian with a sense of humour. However, that's a smaller percentage of the population than the Welsh account for.

What you're actually being asked for is some flattery. When asking you what brought you to the province, a British Columbian actually wants you to validate their view of BC as the finest place on earth to live. Again, depending on your location, you could end up causing offence. You'll want to be careful.

For example, saying "I love trees" in the Lower Mainland, the southern half of Vancouver Island, and the Gulf Islands means you consider trees to be living creatures worthy of safeguarding and that they must be preserved and protected at any cost.

The rest of the province doesn't tend to anthropomorphize inanimate objects, so saying "I love trees" means you love cutting them down in order to make a living and provide for your family.

And "Isle of Trees" is what Vancouver Island, Pender Island, Galiano Island, Gabriola Island, and Mayne Island call themselves when they're in a good mood. Saturna Island favours "Isle of Whales." Salt Spring Island prefers "Isle of Money."[4]

Pay attention to your surroundings. If you find yourself in Northern BC, where the main occupations are in resource-based industries, you don't want people to think you're a Coastie. Or worse, a leftie. This has nothing to do with politics; they just have a deep and abiding antipathy to left-handed people in that part of the province, due to the number of serious industrial accidents when a left-handed logger attempts to use a right-handed Husqvarna.

If you end up in any urban environment—excepting Kamloops—where people like to believe that the fair trade ethical coffee beans they are grinding for use in the Brass and Copper ERG8 La Pavoni Europiccola were delivered by leprechauns riding unicorns you don't want people to think you even know that a Husqvarna is a brand of professional-grade

---

4   If you sound this out, you'll get an extra additional bonus joke.

chainsaw used by lumberjacks. Helpful hint: You can dress like a lumberjack; you just can't really be one. Oh, and if you know that the ERG8 La Pavoni Europiccola is a brand of professional-grade espresso machines, don't mention it in, say, Williams Lake.

Oddly, no matter what region of the province you're in, if people ask what you do, you can tell them, "Oh, I'm just here shooting whales" without any repercussions. British Columbians will either assume you're a documentarian or that you hunt them for sport, depending, again, on just where you are when you make that statement. Either way, it's a safe conversational gambit.

You can also talk about gardening. Even in the heart of a concrete jungle (so, Burnaby) the residents of British Columbia like to grow things. And, no, I'm not going to make a "grow-op" joke here. Compared to the rest of Canada, BC is a lush, verdant paradise. Even the cold parts. It's the only place in the country where "urban farmer" is not used as a pejorative.

Once you know how to converse, you'll be able to pick up on the nuanced subtleties of language used in BC. This will be a real asset to you as you purchase transactional goods and services (covered in Chapter Nine and Chapter Ten) or if you are seeking companionship and fellowship (Chapter Twelve), and, although speaking British Columbian may take a bit of effort, it will be worth it in the end, and, more important, it will keep you safe.

Oh, one more thing. The word "Tsawwassen" is from the North Straits Salish language and means "your ferry is delayed." It is pronounced exactly the way it is spelled.

3　How to Spot a Local

SURVIVING BY IDENTIFYING

BC is a popular destination. A lot of people come here. You're not alone. Although there will be times you wish you were. And you will meet a lot of folks who create an initial impression of being locals, but who are actually visitors or newcomers just like you are. It's important to be able to quickly identify a true British Columbian from an aspirational one.

This chapter will help you avoid wasting your time interacting with someone who, just like you, is still trying to figure the place out.

The first thing you will observe is how many different cultures make up British Columbia. BC is the most multicultural province in Canada, which shouldn't surprise you if you're reading this book in order (since I mentioned in the previous chapter that many British Columbians do not speak either English or French as their first language). You could be skimming the book or perhaps running away from a bookstore clerk or mall security guard, however, so let me explain in more detail.

Over one-quarter of the population of British Columbia (30.3% in metric) are visible minorities and about 5% (one-twentieth) of the population are Aboriginal. And there are many communities in the province where the term "visible minority" should have sardonic quotation marks around the word "minority."

Here, again in more or less descending order, are the cities in BC that have the highest proportion of "visible minorities":

1) Richmond, with 76.3% of the population identifying as a visible minority.

2) Burnaby, where 63.6% of the population identify as a visible minority.

3) Surrey has 58.5% of its population identifying as a visible minority.

4) Coquitlam maintains a 50.2% visible minority rate.

5) New Westminster, with 38.9% of the population identifying as visible minorities.

6) West Vancouver, with 36.4% more or less tied with . . .

7) Delta, with 36% of the population, followed by,

8) Victoria, at 27.7%, and

9) Oak Bay, coming in at 15% of the population identifying as visible minorities, but only if you include "Welsh."

So the word "minority" really only applies in New West, West Van, Delta, Victoria, and Oak Bay. The city of Vancouver has a visible minority rate of 51.6% and Metro Vancouver (also called the Greater Vancouver Area, which is an oxymoron, surely) averages out to 67.3%, which explains why they have the most ethnically diverse hockey riots.

This diversity is great for, you know, inclusion and culture and tolerance and whatnot, but does make things more difficult when you just want to figure out who is a local and who is not.

If you were visiting Korea, say (and I'm going to assume you'd be in South Korea, unless you booked with a really bad travel agent or used a really sketchy website), and you wanted to talk to a local, you'd glance around for someone who, you know, looks Korean. Travelling in France? Just say *Bonjour, comment ça va?* to the nearest person. If they insult your dialect and pronunciation, they are *un vrai citoyen français*. Newcomer to Wales? Anybody named Taffy who tries to steal from you is a safe bet for advice on local attractions and restaurant recommendations. Just hang onto your fanny pack. And call it a "belt bag" when you're in the UK.

It doesn't work that way in British Columbia. It's hard to spot an honest-to-goodness real local British Columbian. You will want to be able to recognize and relate to the people you meet and utilize the correct nomenclature you learned in the previous chapter.

Here then are the six most commonly encountered types of British Columbians. Assume, unless otherwise indicated, that these categories of locals can come in any skin tone and from any ethnic background. You will notice they are often defined by opposition to each other: hippies to hipsters, tree huggers to loggers, oil field workers to pipeline protesters.

Hippies and Hipsters

Let's begin with Hippies. Britain had the Swinging Sixties, and London in particular had Soho and Carnaby Street. The United States had the Summer of Love, and the intersection of Haight and Ashbury Streets in San Francisco. In Canada, British Columbia was the epicentre of the counterculture movement in the 1960s, with Vancouver's Kitsilano neighbourhood being Ground Zero for the great hippie heyday, specifically, 4th Avenue West, where, in 1968, the Naam Restaurant opened for business, serving vegetarian food twenty-four hours a day, seven days a week, just like a truck-stop diner. Only with fewer truckers and more tofu.

Most of the original hippies drifted away and decided to become Baby Boomers instead. They got well-paying jobs, bought reasonably priced homes, and settled down to enjoy the most demographically advantaged lives in history. Often they ended up back in their original neighbourhoods where once they were young, free, and foolish. Today, 4th Avenue West boasts high-end restaurants, expensive condos, and the inevitable Whole Foods Market. Kind of a metaphor. Although the Naam is still in operation, in the original location no less, still denying capitalism and the principles of the free market by serving tofu, spelt, and what I assumed were twigs and potting soil. *Namaste*!

In British Columbia you can find authentic hippies in Nelson, a town founded by Quakers and later inundated with draft dodgers and deserters. Tofino has draft dodgers and surfers. And all of the Gulf Islands are a good place to play "spot the hippie," with Salt Spring also offering a good selection of retired rock stars. You can also find real-deal hippies in Victoria's James Bay and Fernwood neighbourhoods, as well as at poetry readings, protests, and potluck suppers. Hippies really know how to put the "pot" in a potluck.

Genuine British Columbia hippies are easy to pick out in a crowd. Look for men with beards, bald spots (*en français: cheveux dégarnis*), and ponytails, or women with braids or buns (*en français: chignon du cou*) or ponytails. They are often, but not always, aging, so the hair will be grey. They will be wearing sandals, which won't single them out, and handmade tie-dye shirts, which will. Maybe a vest from India, cotton harem pants from White Rock, and a dreamcatcher necklace from Cheryl's Trading Post. Possibly coveralls. Definitely support stockings. This applies to either gender. The whole outfit, I mean. If they happen to be younger hippies, which are actually a thing here in BC, they will look and dress the same as their elders, but both the grey hair and tie dye will be ironic.

Speaking of ironic, let's talk Hipsters. Hipsters are not modern versions of hippies. They're worse. And they are worse off. Poor dears. All hipsters are millennials, although not all millennials are hipsters. Hipsters like to express their individuality by dressing and thinking exactly the same as every other hipster, so they are easy to identify, although female hipsters have a bit more leeway regarding fashion. They might wear skinny jeans that are blue, skinny jeans that are black, or tights in lieu of jeans. They could wear either a baggy plaid shirt or an oversized sweater. The sweater could have a picture of a cute animal on it or a sarcastic quote. It could even have a sarcastic animal picture on it. Or a cute quotation. It's all about the freedom to make choices. Possibly a gender-neutral fragrance. Definitely black-framed Kendall Round Readers, with or without a prescription.

The male hipster will dress so uniformly you could be forgiven for assuming there is only one of them in the entire province and he keeps following you around. There's the beard, the man bun, the skinny jeans, the suspenders, the doeskin, and the toque. The toque may or may not have a pompom. That's it. That's the look. And I'm not engaging in hyperbole here; they really do all look exactly the same. Recently a hipster sued the *Massachusetts Institute of Technology Review* for running his photo alongside an online article without his permission. Turned out it wasn't him. In other words, the guy who sued couldn't tell the difference between a photograph of himself and a photograph of a completely different person. The article was titled

"The Hipster Effect: Why anti-conformists always end up looking the same." Now that's ironic.

Hipsters flourish in British Columbia, because diversity. Hipsters believe in diversity, just not diversity of opinion. This is a direct result of social media. It's all algorithms all the time, baby, which tends to create confirmation bias and echo chambers. Hipsters spend a lot of time on Instagram, which I assume is their preferred unit of measurement; Tumblr, which I know is a setting on my washing machine; and Twitter, which at least sounds like something you'd hear in a natural, as opposed to a virtual, environment. And, yeah, I know I sound like the "you kids get off my lawn" old guy (which I totally am) but I believe the online world contributes to their innate unhappiness and dissatisfaction and their unique combination of equal parts self-absorption and self-loathing. Everyone posts about their perfect lives but none of it is actually true, let alone real. The hipster generation earns less, spends more, and doesn't have the same opportunities the hippie generation did. The imaginary internet world just seems unnecessarily cruel on top of all that.

Where to find a hipster, you ask? Well, if you order a caffè latte, your barista is likely to be a hipster. But you really should think about cutting back. So is your bartender. You really should think about Cutty Sark. Walk into a gaming store or a comic book shop and you'll get "served" (one more time for the deliberate use of quotation marks, this time to make the point that customer service is, at best, a theoretical concept) by a hipster. They are store clerks, computer programmers, and, sometimes, small business owners—if that business is a retro barbershop, a craft brewery, or a gourmet food truck.

Hipsters, by the way, hate being called "hipsters," and they also hate being described as "millennials," although these are interchangeable if not intersectional terms. Case in

44

point: I referred to a young lady as a hipster, because I'm a horrible person, and she corrected me with "I'm a millennial, we don't like labels." She might have been attempting irony.

You can find hipsters in every major city in British Columbia, even Kamloops, as well as smaller towns and villages. The smaller the community, the more forlorn the hipster, but they are everywhere.

Tree Huggers and Loggers

At any given time in the province of British Columbia, one half of the population is chained to a tree and the other half is trying to cut it down. As you will learn in the final chapter of this book, British Columbians love themselves a good old protest. The environmental movement in particular has a long and contentious history. The credit, or the blame, for this can be attributed to the hippies. They started it. Tree Huggers is a term used to describe people involved in anti-logging activism. So, a badge of honour or backhanded compliment, depending on which side you were on during the War of the Woods or the Liberation of Clayoquot Sound.

How will you recognize a tree hugger? If you stumble onto a protest march, and this will happen if you spend more than a weekend anywhere in BC, quickly check to see what the folks marching are all riled up about. If you see the words "clear cut" on any banner or sign and hear folk music, you're in luck—you'll be able to introduce yourself to authentic British Columbia tree huggers. Try not to let the smell of patchouli, marijuana, or nostalgia get to you. If you hear people shouting "We were robbed" or complaining about the Canucks penalty kill, you aren't at a protest. A hockey riot is about to break out. Run.

All hippies are tree huggers, but not all tree huggers are hippies. Tree huggers come in all shapes and sizes. They look like anybody and everybody. Senior citizens, students, moms, dads, tall people, short people, Asians, South Asians, Caucasians, Aboriginals ... although hipsters will be underrepresented because it's hard to get a good Wi-Fi signal in the woods.

The term Loggers is used to describe people who work in British Columbia's forestry industry. All lumberjacks are loggers, but not all loggers are lumberjacks. The forest sector is the fifth-largest industry in the province, the largest producer of softwood lumber in North America, and responsible for over a third of all provincial exports; contributes over 12 billion dollars towards British Columbia's economy; and directly employs almost 60,000 people, none of whom you will meet at a pro-logging rally,[1] because, you know, they've got jobs.

Most of British Columbia is covered in trees: 64% of the province is forested, which translates into an area greater in size than the entire state of Texas. That's a lot of trees. And a lot of folks who support logging and rely on it for support, and who come in all shapes and sizes and look like everybody and anybody. Senior citizens, students, moms, dads, tall people, short people, Asians, South Asians, Caucasians, Aboriginals ...

If you want to meet loggers, head to a logging town, a pulp mill town, or any shopping mall. You can also run into tree huggers and hipsters in these very same locations, so be aware of the differences. Both groups wear a lot of plaid, but loggers will also wear tartan. Loggers don't wear skinny jeans, because there's no place to put their tools. Loggers will not use moustache wax. Loggers don't sport man buns,[2] but will go old-school with a "business at the front, party at the back" haircut. Not hairstyle. And both groups will do their best to shop local, but with loggers this includes shopping at their local Canadian Tire.

46

---

1   Rare to the point of being nonexistent.
2   Man buns are just mullets for millennials.

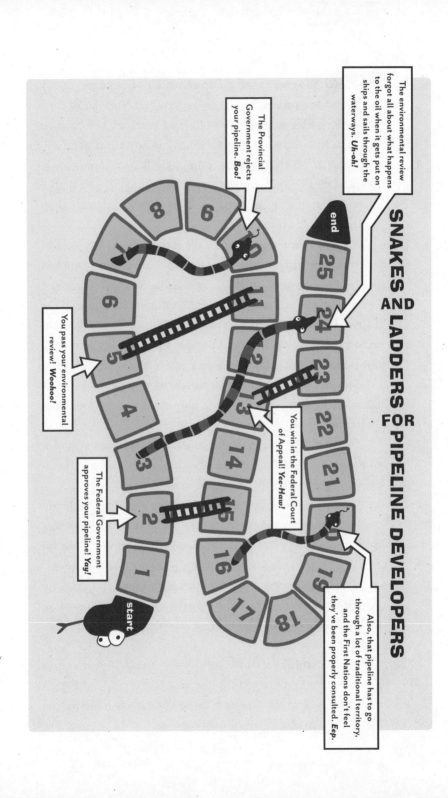

Oil-field Workers and Pipeline Protestors

If, instead of a protest march, you encounter a blockade, then you will be able to meet both Oil-field Workers, who will be on one side of the barricade, and Pipeline Protestors, who will be at the drum circle on the other side. If you thought loggers and tree huggers didn't like each other, hooh-boy, there's more common ground between Norway and Ecuador than there is between these two groups ...

Pipeline protestors are a little newer to the resistance/grievance/dissentient scene, but they're making good time and really putting in a lot of effort, considering how much harder it is to chain yourself to a pipeline. All of them want to stop the Trans Mountain Pipeline Expansion, most of them also want to halt the LNG Pipeline, and some of them would like to shut down the Massey Tunnel because it sort of looks like a pipeline.

Hippies are often underrepresented at pipeline protests because the drum circles won't play any Country Joe & the Fish tunes.

Now for a philosophical statement. There are two types of people in the world: those who divide the world into two types of people and those who do not.

In British Columbia, though, the two types of people are those on opposite sides of the renewable resource management, renewable resource extraction, or environmental apocalyptic pillaging debate. Talk about your two solitudes.

This division even applies to tree huggers and pipeline protestors. Really, you ask? Seriously, you say? Eyebrow, you arch? Both groups are environmentalists. Surely they are like-minded and unified.

I used to think so, and I even believed that a Venn diagram about the two groups would just look like a circle, maybe a circle drawn with an unsteady hand but a circle nonetheless. There'd be an absurd amount of overlap.

Here's the thing. I also thought the same about the relationship between tree huggers and bicycle lane proponents. Then the city of Victoria cut down a tree to make way for a new bike lane and, geez, did folks ever choose sides. Reading the comments in the local media was sort of like watching *Alien vs. Predator*. Both sides were terrifying in their certitude, and I didn't know who to root for.

At some point, some issue will come up that will cause tree huggers and pipeline protestors to turn against each other. Maybe the tree huggers will decide that placards and protest signs should all be hand-woven to save timber, maybe the pipeline protestors will try to curtail the use of oil-based Magic Markers and Sharpies, maybe David Suzuki will issue an *indicere bellum edictum* . . . [3] Who knows? When it does happen, though, it will be a bigger seismic event than the long-awaited massive super-thrust earthquake—and will probably cause more damage.

Myself, I think the two types of people in the world are those who shower before going to work and those who shower after work. There are also people who don't shower. They prefer a nice hot soak in a tub. This is either a way to relax or a waste of water, depending on your environmental sensitivities.

Point is, be careful when approaching British Columbians. It's hard to tell, from appearance, just which side of the Great Divide they may be on. That woman in the cargo pants, work boots, and a lumberjack shirt could be a renowned performance artist or a farm wife wearing sensible shoes. For your own well-being, make sure that she notices your "I Love Trees" button either way. That long-haired, bearded man muttering nonsense and stumbling toward you could be either homeless (an "underprivileged thoroughfare resident") or a professor

49

---

3   Or possibly a *surrexerunt ludere protestatus*. Depending on his mood.

emeritus from the Creative Writing Department at Simon Fraser University. All things being equal, for your own safety, you should give him a loonie. Do not say, "Hey, here's a loonie for a loony," however, unless you are in the Fraser Valley, where this behaviour is not only accepted but encouraged.

Here's the real secret to identifying an actual British Columbian, regardless of age, ethnicity, gender, or politics. Whereas a newcomer to the province could be in a pulp mill town like Ocean Falls, a logging community like Lumby, or a hipster haven like Kelowna, and be openly astonished and delighted by the variety of both the scenery and people, a true British Columbian, despite the fact they live in an environmental, economic, and cultural paradise, will look unhappy.

4 Dress for Success

SURVIVING THE FASHION

Now that you know where British Columbia is located (to the left of Alberta) and how to get there, and you've figured out that speaking with British Columbians means not saying anything that might cause offence (or not saying anything at all beyond "I love trees" and "Forgive me") and, of course, how to tell an outsider (filled with enthusiasm and interest) from a local (full of resentment and ennui), it's now time to learn the important lesson of how to look like a local. After all, it doesn't help to speak the language, know the culture, or understand the unwritten rules of a place if you dress like a rube.

Here's the first thing you need to know about local fashion. British Columbia is the worst-dressed province in Canada. This is not just my opinion. This is based on surveys, scientifically conducted polls, and statistics.[1]

British Columbians do understand what the word "aesthetic" means. They are able to apply aesthetics to everything from their ornamental gardens to their decorative parks to their fetching architecture. Not, alas, to their fashion. They have a sense of entitlement; they lack a sense of style.

51

---

1   And math.

Yes, there are high-end boutiques, luxury clothing brands, and expensive shoe stores in every city in BC. Maybe even Kamloops. Don't be fooled. Those businesses are purely for the tourist trade. You can browse in them, you can even purchase clothes or accessories there, but you will not end up looking like you belong.

"How can this be?" I hear you ask. How could British Columbia be considered the worst-dressed province? Surely a potash miner or an alfalfa farmer from Saskatchewan would have a poorer sense of style? Or a rig worker or cattle rancher from Alberta? What about Newfoundland and/or Labrador? Someone stepping off a lobster dory isn't going to be an example of sartorial splendour, right?

Certainly, a shipbuilder from Tatamagouche, Nova Scotia, or a fishing guide at Lake Pekwachnamaykoskwaskwaypinwanik (and you thought Tsawwassen was hard to pronounce), Manitoba, isn't going to be any more or any less well-dressed than a fabricator from Stoner, British Columbia.

That's not how a province's style is determined. It's not based on how regular, hard-working, small-town, salt-of-the-earth folks dress; it's based on the appearance of the people who live and work in the biggest, most sophisticated city. Quebec isn't stylish, but Montreal is. Ontario? Full of civil servants (who are neither civil nor servile, let alone fashionable), but the fashionistas of Toronto more than make up for them. In a recent online survey, 84.3% of *female* respondents selected Edmonton men as the best dressed in the country. Alberta: it's not just cowboys anymore.

In other words, British Columbia's reputation rests on the fashion choices of its largest, most cosmopolitan metropolis: Vancouver. This is what drags down the rating of the entire province. Their fashion police were all busted by internal affairs.

Vancouver is the worst-dressed city in Canada. And, on a global ranking, Vancouver is the third worst-dressed city in the world. This is according to *Flare* magazine, who should know, and *GQ* magazine, who should know better. So, con-gratulations, Vancouver, you've earned a bronze medal in dressage.

Here, this time in ascending order, are the worst-dressed cities on the entire earth:

1) Orlando, Florida, USA
2) Maui, Hawaii, USA
3) Vancouver, British Columbia, Canada
4) Harajuku, Tokyo Prefecture, Japan
5) Boston, Massachusetts, USA
6) Seattle, Washington, USA
7) San Francisco, California, USA
8) Ottawa, Ontario, Canada
9) Pittsburgh, Pennsylvania, USA

The coastal neighbourhood of New Jersey known as The Jersey Shore came in at 10th place. Remember the eponymous television series (and harbinger of The End Times) that aired on MTV[2] back when Barack Obama was the US president? That neighbourhood and those people are better dressed than Vancouverites. Seven times better. I think that's how math works. I could be wrong.

Now, surprisingly, most of the cities on this list weren't happy about their inclusion or the methodology used to arrive at the results. Ottawa is used to finishing in 8th place, so they just collectively shrugged and resumed watching both types of Senators not do their jobs.

53

2   Once the network decided to ignore the first letter in its name.

When the article was originally published in *GQ* it didn't cause a fuss in Vancouver at all. Surprising, eh? Wonder why? Is it because Vancouverites are thick-skinned and slow to take offence? Nope. Is it because they have a healthy self-regard? Uh-uh. Is it because the citizens of Vancouver have a sense of humour? That's not it.

Nobody in Vancouver got upset because nobody in Vancouver reads *GQ*. People in Vancouver don't pick up fashion magazines. For the same reason I don't buy fitness magazines. What would be the point?

Then MSN Travel picked up the article and, yup, it went viral, and you bet Vancouver got upset. The author of the original article, Vivian Song, was taken to task. Not by everybody, mind; some Vancouverites chose not to blame the messenger. Instead they blamed Chip Wilson.

Now perhaps he deserves some of the blame for founding his ridiculously successful "athletic apparel company." And for coining the phrase "athleisure wear." Maybe. There's some debate about that. But nobody is forcing government workers to show up for work bedecked in Lululemon. (Yoga pants aren't pants, people. They're tights. Tights, dammit!) There is no bylaw anywhere in the Metro Vancouver Area making this an enforceable dress code. Appearances to the contrary notwithstanding.

And that English as a Second Language instructor heading off to the food court to hold class sporting the same puffy down vest worn by Marty McFly in *Back to the Future*? They don't have to wear that. Just because Michael J. Fox hails from Burnaby doesn't make him a trendsetter. And that movie came out in 1985.

British Columbia is full of contrarians and individualists, and part of the unique and independent nature of the province is their refusal to follow the rules. This applies to how they dress. Oddly, this distinctiveness creates a sort of "let's put on our clothes to start the day in accordance with the whims of the weather" collectivism, the equivalent of Mao jackets in Communist China, only with more natural fabrics.

So you won't have to spend a lot of time dressing for the day, although you can spend a lot of money. Looking like you bought most of your clothing at a thrift store doesn't mean you'll be paying thrift store prices.

Let's start with fashion advice for the men. Gentlemen, take a look at the helpful accompanying illustration and you'll see what you can get away with looking like in the province of BC.

You will not want to dress like a hipster. It's one thing to fit in; it's another to be mistaken for some other guy. You'll end up signing for their registered mail and having to deal with threatening correspondence from the student loan collection agency.

Having said that, even among non-hipsters, you'll notice an abundance of plaid. The entire province looks like Chris Cornell never died and grunge was still a thing. When Neil Young shows up[3] even he's like, "Dial it back a bit, man." So you'll need to pick up a flannel shirt or two.

You won't need to invest any money in skinny jeans; simply pick up a comfortable pair of Wranglers or some relaxed-fit khakis at Value Village and you'll fit in anywhere in the province. When the weather turns nice, shorts are the best option. By shorts I mean beige cargo shorts, the kind with enough pockets to serve as a de facto utility belt. Shorts can be worn with sandals or shoes. The knee-high black socks are optional unless you are over 50 years of age, at which point they are compulsory.

You never know a man until you walk in his shoes. In British Columbia those shoes will be hiking boots. Probably Timberlands. Although in milder weather you can wear sandals. But only Birkenstocks. Never a Fluevog. Only three men

55

---

3   For a concert or a protest.

doeskin jacket

bike helmet

SHARE THE ROAD

long hipster beard

marijuana leaf tattoo

man bun

cargo shorts with lots of pockets

hiking boots

knee-high black socks

anorak-type jacket

sandals

metal reusable water bottle

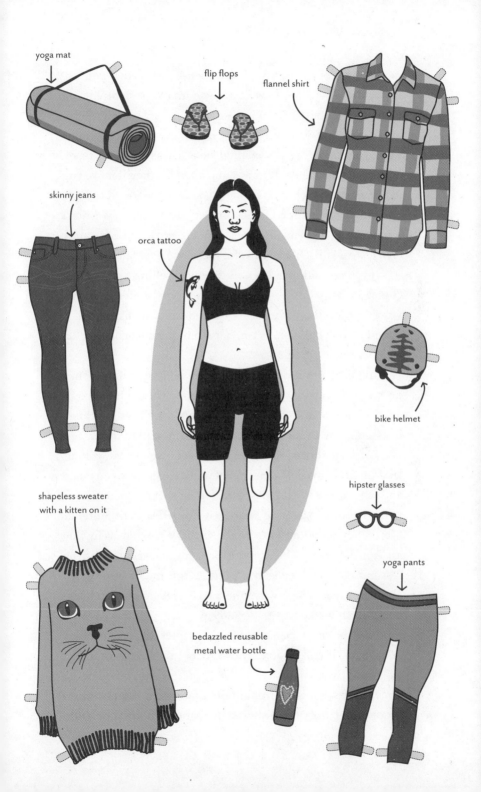

in the entire province wear designer shoes, and if you ask them, they'll tell you how tired they are of constantly being mistaken for tourists.

You will also want to invest in a rainproof jacket. Don't waste your money on a "water-repellent" jacket. The only repellent thing about them is how damp and cold they'll make you feel. Rainproof jackets won't keep you much warmer, though, so spring for the lining. Or buy yourself a turtleneck if you don't mind feeling like you are being slowly, gently, and constantly choked to death. Quick! Time for the Heineken Manoeuvre!

If you're visiting in the winter and travelling to the colder climes of BC, you should pick up a warm winter coat that you can combine with the shorts and the sandals. This is a common look because, as you'll learn in the next chapter, the weather is awfully changey.

You'll be pleased to note that you will be saving money on hair gel, shaving cream, and cologne. Although I encourage you not to swap out your deodorant for a crystal dipped in essential oils. Causes chafing. Your armpits will thank me.

For formal occasions you could get a shapeless, colourless suit. By colourless I mean that weird shade between taupe and tan. Pick one up at the thrift store or spend a lot of money at the nearest Expensive Shapeless Colourless Suit Store for Men. They'll end up looking the same. Wrinkled. Why buy an iron when you have more pressing concerns? And by "formal occasion" I mean a protest. You might be worried about how you'll look when the television cameras catch you being perp-walked to the paddy wagon. Also, never, ever, ever use the term "paddy wagon." Chapter Two, remember? Police van. Patrol wagon. Welsh school bus. All acceptable. Not "paddy wagon."

Mostly, though, a Mountain Equipment Co-op waterproof jacket worn with shorts and sandals is suitable attire for any occasion. You can also wear a bike helmet with any ensemble, just not when you're actually bicycling.

Now some fashion advice for the ladies. I'll give you a moment to process that statement. Go ahead, roll your eyes, toss this book across the room (or directly at the pursuing bookstore clerk), and grumble, "Who does he think he is?" You can also use "He's got a lot of nerve," or "How dare he?" I understand. Get it out of your system. I can wait.

Let me confess that I'm not a fashion plate. I'm not even a fashion finger bowl. On my best days I'm barely presentable. This is one of the reasons I now make my home in British Columbia. I arrived here, looked around, and realized that, for the first time in my entire adult life, I wasn't the worst-dressed person in my immediate vicinity. The whole place dressed badly. It was a liberating and life-affirming moment.

I'm completely and totally unqualified to offer fashion advice to women. Like most men. Actually, I'm probably even less qualified than most men. But I'm not offering real advice. It's not real fashion. This is how women dress in British Columbia. I'm trying to help you blend in.

Now, if you also take a look at the helpful illustration that accompanies this chapter you will notice that women have more choices than men. Regarding clothing, that is. This isn't the time or the place to discuss paternalism, misogyny, or historical oppression, all of which I am even less qualified to weigh in on than women's fashion.

You will not want to emulate the hipsters either. You don't want to walk around in a sweater embroidered with a Frida Kahlo self-portrait, even if it reads "I like people too much or not at all." First of all, nobody can carry off that look. Second of all, that's either an unintentional or deliberate misquote. Sylvia Plath said that.

Skinny jeans are still an option, though. Also leggings or tights, although if you decide you don't want to wear Lululemon, you should still carry a fluorescently coloured yoga mat with you at all times. Rolled up, it makes a handy pillow. You can unroll it on the beach and it will be way more comfortable and easier to get the sand out of than a towel or blanket. And if a yoga class spontaneously breaks out, you'll be prepared.

You never know a woman until you walk in her shoes. In British Columbia those shoes will be Skechers. In warmer weather? They also make a sandal. Never heels, unless you want to spend all your time fending off advances from local guys who really want to meet an out-of-towner.

You'll also want a rainproof jacket, which could look like a trench coat or an anorak or even a poncho. Way more options than the men have.

If you only take one piece of advice from this chapter, take this: BC may not be fancy, but it's active. You'll need a good sports bra. You'll be hiking, biking, and climbing. Activities are fun to British Columbians. They may be the worst-dressed province, but they are also the fittest. Be prepared. And make good use of your time and abilities.

If you go to the Travel BC website and look up what to wear for your trip they will actually caution you to leave valuables and what they call "dressy clothes" behind unless you're coming for a formal event. So even the official government travel and tourism departments acknowledge the casual relationship British Columbians have with fashion. What they don't tell you is what you *should* wear for formal occasions. Say you've been asked to attend a "public affirmation of love and togetherness," or "wedding." A shapeless, brightly patterned dress partnered with a jean jacket will be appropriate. If you're in the bridal party, then the jean jacket will have rhinestones.[4] Either way, you can also wear your bicycle helmet.

I have no advice regarding cleansers, foundations, conditioners, exfoliates nor defoliants, face creams, hand creams, or even ice cream. All I can tell you is that every product you use for your daily regimen comes available in British Columbia in an organic free-range fair-trade version that emulsifies and detoxifies. And doesn't actually, you know, work. Helpful hint: Maybe keep using the same stuff you're used to, but cover the bottle (or tubs or vials or whatever) with labels from the locally sourced handcrafted naturopathic versions. And, as a money-saving tip, I'm pretty sure those artisans still get their cut as long as the product leaves the store. Always happy to help you stretch your dollar.

Also worthy of note, in many regions of BC (most of the Gulf Islands, much of Victoria, Kitsilano obviously, Crofton surprisingly) hair dye is unavailable or even illegal, unless it is in bright shades of purple, turquoise, or magenta. So, if your hair is turning silver and you'd rather people didn't notice, you might want to check first. It's one thing to rinse away the grey; it's another to look like you suffered a horrible Kool-Aid explosion.

One final piece of advice for the ladies regarding jewellery and such. Anything goes. Your necklaces, earrings, belts, purses, and piercings will all be admired and accepted. Just don't tell anybody where you actually purchased them. If someone admires your, I dunno, silver brooch? Is that a thing? Anyway. Tell them you got it from a thrift store for 2 bucks. In British Columbia, women brag about how little they spend. It's a status symbol.

Now, for both male and female readers, the one fashion accessory, the one must-have you absolutely should carry

---

4   Or it might be bedazzled. Options.

with you at all times is a reusable water bottle. Not one of the plastic ones, you earth-destroying whale-hating turtle-killing outsider; no, sir, you want one of those silver metal vacuum insulated babies personalized with your name engraved on it. Just remember, if anybody asks, it didn't cost you an outrageous amount of money (seriously, they can range from a reasonable $13.60 for an entry-level Custom Water Canada model to an outrageous $384.80 for a Rockit Claw Stone Grey Stainless Steel "fresh drink system." So you'd drop almost 400 bucks to carry around potable water and maybe save the environment? Think about it. Has the environment really earned that sort of investment?), you picked it up at the Sally Ann. And the name etched onto it? Just a coincidence. That's when you knew you had to buy it. I mean, what are the odds? Also, only 2 bucks! Can you believe it?

Oh, and if the strictures regarding clothing seem to be unfathomably complex, you can solve this by hanging out (literally) someplace where nobody wears clothes.

Here, in order of historical importance, are the top five nude beaches in British Columbia:

1) **Wreck Beach, Vancouver:** steps away from the University of British Columbia undergraduate on-campus housing. Giving students a real education since 1991.

2) **Ram Creek Hot Springs:** a provincially protected ecological preserve in the Skookumchuck with nude bathers whenever the park rangers aren't around.

3) **Crescent Beach, Surrey:** the mayor of Surrey is tired of getting complaints and the city may shut it down soon, so you may want to go sooner rather than later. Or if you picked this book up in a used book store in 2040, then

they've already shut it down. Sorry. Also Prime Minister Ivy Mulroney is doing a terrific job managing the whole illegal alien issue.[5]

4) **Barnston Island:** worth the time for the ferry ride from Surrey across Parson's Channel. The ferry is free and the sand on this beach rivals anything you'd find in Santa Monica or Puerto Vallarta. Not technically a nude beach, locals refer to it alliteratively as the Barnston Bare Beach, which just makes it sound adorable.

5) **Little Tribune Bay:** Hornby Island's clothing-optional beach, although all of Hornby is more or less clothing-optional, particularly when gardening. Nude Gardening Day is year-round.

So your choices, or Hobson's choice, are to be poorly dressed or barely dressed. You'll want to wear flip-flops in either case because of sand mites.

For those of you who don't think clothing should be optional, I'd like to assure you that if you carefully follow the advice in this chapter, you will dress appropriately and not stand out. Even better, with a little thought, a bit of effort, and an almost complete lack of self-esteem, you may even be able to pass for a genuine British Columbian. At least as far as your "outerwear" is concerned. Your "inner where," the emotions and thoughts you keep deep inside that make up your true personality, will remain unchanged.

Unless you join a yoga class.

Your "outlook" will stay the same until you attend your first protest march.

---

5   In the future? Actual aliens.

5 It's a Damp Cold

SURVIVING THE WEATHER

As noted in the introduction to this book, what other parts of the world call "a disaster," British Columbians call "weather." In BC you can experience blizzards, heat waves, and monsoons, often in the same location and even on the same day. The weather is, as I've mentioned, "changey." That applies from the most northerly part of the province, where winter actually occurs on an annual basis and most of the precipitation comes in frozen form, to the Lower Mainland and the southern tip of Vancouver Island where most of the precipitation is of the moist variety and it almost never, ever snows except when it does that one time of the year, every year, catching everyone off guard and sending the citizenry into a state of shock.

I had lived in Victoria for almost an entire winter before I experienced what, in other parts of Canada, would be a light dusting of snow. It floated down gently from the sky, like powdered sugar sprinkled on a Lee's Doughnuts donut. It was enough to wreak havoc on traffic and infrastructure. The city shut down. A state of emergency wasn't officially declared, but a state of panic ensued. I grew up in northern Alberta. I wasn't frightened. I was prepared for snow. I went next door to ask my neighbour if I could borrow his snow shovel.[1] He didn't own one. "Don't worry," he said, 'it'll just melt off by tomorrow." This struck me as a bit irresponsible, and also, who doesn't own a snow shovel? "It never snows here," he said. "And yet," I said, indicating the current situation with the sort of half-shrug/half-wave gesture meant to indicate mild reproach. He just smiled. "You call this snow?" Then he shut his door.

I decided to hedge my bets. I didn't actually purchase a snow shovel. Why spend the money if it never snows? No point in going to extremes. I did, however, spend several hours with my kitchen broom, an extension cord, and a hair dryer making sure my stairs and sidewalk were completely free of snow. I felt smugly superior and slightly judgmental of the rest of the neighbourhood, none of whom did anything at all to clear their walks. The next morning all the snow had melted away. Who doesn't own a snow shovel? This guy. Why not? Why bother?

It wasn't until this very year, when we got ten whole days of actual winter, almost like Real Canada, complete with snow that stuck around and temperatures below freezing that I finally made the trek of shame to Canadian Tire and picked up a proper snow shovel. On the way back from the store it occurred to me that I already owned a leaf rake, a garden spade, and a locally fabricated composting scoop made of organic bamboo and reclaimed hemp, any of which would have done an adequate job of clearing away snow, even if it wasn't part of their original job description. For a guy who grew up in northern Alberta, it was embarrassing. The snow shovel does do a better job of picking up the cherry blossom detritus than the rake did, though, so it was a good purchase anyway. And if I wanted to live in Real Canada, I'd move back

65

---

[1] So my definition of "prepared" is a little loose. Sue me.

to Real Canada. There's a reason I moved to Victoria. And that reason is weather.

Real born-and-bred British Columbians, especially those who live in the more populated areas of the province, like to remind the residents of Real Canada that, for the most part, Real Winter doesn't Really Happen here. They do this by posting videos of themselves mowing the lawn in February. Or photographs of their rhododendrons blooming and/or their tulips opening. In March. Or a simple tweet announcing the final score of the annual April flower count. This is known as Meteorological Snobbery.

Then, when it does snow, these same people go online with the question: "What is this white stuff falling from the sky?" To which Real Canada replies: "Karma."

In British Columbia, anywhere north of Hope on the mainland or above the Malahat on the Island, where it gets cold and snowy during December and January, the seasons are: Actual Winter, Genuine Spring, Let's Catch the BC Lions Game (Summer), and Snow Tires Suddenly Required (Fall). In the Lower Mainland and the southern part of Vancouver Island, where December and January are cold and rainy, the seasons are: Kinda Winter, Almost Spring (also known as Still Raining season), Sorta Summer (also known as Delays Caused by Roadway Construction season), and Raining Again (Fall).

In British Columbia, a weather forecast can be "rain followed by showers," "showers followed by rain," "showers mixed with rain, followed by snow," or, occasionally, "showers followed by fog, followed by hail, followed by sunny breaks." I'm not kidding about the fog. The West Coast Fog Zone is the actual (and appropriate) name for a three-kilometre-wide stretch running from Port Hardy on the eastern tip of Vancouver Island all the way around the western perimeter as far south as Port Renfrew. It's considered to be a separate microclimate, possibly a microaggression, depending on your desire to actually see a mountain peak peeking through the clouds. BC is the only place where humidity automatically comes with precipitation.

Scientists would have you believe there are three types of rainfall: convectional, where warm surface temperatures cause air to heat, rise through the atmosphere, and condense; orographic, which occurs when air has to go up and over a mountain range causing adiabatic cooling, and ultimately condensation; and stratiformic, which, of course, comes from nimbostratus clouds. We all understand this. It's common knowledge.

In British Columbia, however, there are six additional types of rain:

1) **Indeterminate rain:** this is the rain that starts falling without any warning, often on a clear and sunny day. If you go back inside to grab an umbrella, it will stop. If you forget your umbrella, it will start up again. Locals do not consider this to be actual rain.

2) **Sempiternal rain:** this is the rain that starts falling in late September and continues until early December without abatement. Any non-military-grade umbrella will not protect you. Specific to the Lower Mainland, this is exactly what Fox Mulder was complaining about. We'll get to that in a bit.

3) **Exculpatory rain:** this is the rain that starts falling after any unexpected dry and warm period. It occurs just shortly after everybody stops enjoying the weather and begins complaining about being too hot. Known colloquially as "we had it coming" rain, it used to be referred

to as "meritless rain," due to the annual downpour at the now-cancelled Merritt Mountain Music Festival.

4) **Procumbent rain:** this is the rain that starts falling horizontally on windy days and is often mixed with sleet. Also known as "exfoliating rain," any attempt to stay dry will be thwarted when the wind violently inverts your umbrella, snatches it away, and sends it flying. Twelve percent of the refuse in the Great Pacific Garbage Patch consists of umbrellas the trade winds have pilfered from British Columbia.

5) **Unobtrusive rain:** more of a gentle mist or heavy fog, this is the rain that will immediately identify you as an outsider if you comment on it, or, worse, open up an umbrella. In BC, this kind of rain indicates that the outdoor patios are open and available for use.

6) **Appropriate rain:** the exact and correct amount of rain mixed with sunshine to ensure that farmers get enough moisture for their crops and no outdoor events need to be cancelled. Like the Higgs-Boson Particle or Fiscally Accountable Government, it is purely theoretical and has yet to be observed in actuality.

The real lesson to learn is that the parts of the province that don't really get winter don't really get summer. The Okanagan gets cold and snowy during the winter, but more than makes up for it with hot and sunny summers.[2] Lytton is the hottest place in Canada, not because Lyttonians are smoking hot,[3] but as a result of their really, really warm

---

2   Lake Okanagan is also home to British Columbia's version of the Loch Ness Monster, the more approachably named "Ogopogo," no relation to Pogo Possum.
3   They are reasonably attractive.

summers. The average temperature ranges between 28°C, or 82°F, and "Geez, it's hot!" They also set the record for hottest temperature recorded at 44.4°C, or 111°F, or "It burns! It burns! We're all gonna die!" depending on which unit of measurement you'd prefer. Cranbrook doesn't get as hot, but does call itself "the sunniest city in British Columbia," and it's not because of the cheerful dispositions of Cranbrookians. They get more annual sunny days than any other community in the province. Sunny ways, however, are a different matter altogether ... Prince Rupert gets the least amount of sun, being in the heart of the West Coast Fog Zone. Vancouver ... Well, as a resident of Victoria, I like to point out that we get half the annual rainfall that Vancouver gets. An overcast day in Victoria means a cloudy day in Vancouver. If it's cloudy in Victoria, it's raining in Vancouver; if it's raining in Victoria, it's pouring in Vancouver. Weather systems tend to blow over the southern tip of Vancouver Island before crossing the Lower Mainland and running into the North Shore Mountains and slowing down just enough to release any pent-up precipitation. Vancouver is occasionally sundrenched, but usually just drenched.

It rains a lot in Vancouver. It's a sensitive issue. When the *X-Files* moved its filming location from Vancouver back to Los Angeles after five seasons, star David Duchovny, when asked about the move by Conan O'Brien, blamed the weather. "Vancouver is a very nice place if you like 400 inches of rainfall a day," Duchovny said, going on to add, "It's like a tropical rain forest without the tropics." You thought being called the third worst-dressed city in the world got Vancouverites upset? That was nothing compared to the howls of outrage and betrayal this caused. Vancouver doesn't forgive and doesn't forget. Also incapable of taking a joke. Instead of "Welcome to Vancouver: a nuclear weapons free zone," the signs should read "Welcome to Vancouver: we don't think that's funny."

I found out about this controversy just last year. Some alleged actor, a kid really, was shooting a US television series in Vancouver. It was a gritty remake of a beloved '80s sitcom or a gritty reboot of a beloved comic book. Maybe both. I'm torn between "who knows?" and "who cares?" I can't for the life of me remember his name, and I'm not engaged enough to bother looking it up, but the point is, he called Vancouver "boring" and every news outlet and every pundit weighed in … by bringing up David Duchovny's historical insult. Which happened way back in 1997. Some wounds never heal.

Redheads and vampires consider Vancouver to be the Promised Land, that's how little sunshine it gets. And how much rain. Sunglasses are rare to the point of nonexistence. When it's not raining, Vancouverites say, "You can see the mountains." And what other people call "the sun" is referred to as "the giant orb that burns." Also worthy of note: When it's raining cats and dogs you won't be hailing taxis.

However, much like how residents of Victoria try to diminish the quantity and quality of their own precipitation by pointing out that Vancouver has it noticeably worse, Vancouverites will also point out, while being pelted by gale force winds and sheets of rain, that at least they're not in West Vancouver, where things get really bad. This is true. On a rare sunny day in West Vancouver, you can watch retired millionaires shrivel up like prunes and occasionally burst into flames.

In the second chapter of this book I cautioned you against talking about the weather. For your own safety, don't talk about rain. Ever. In the spirit of every Hollywood actor forced to spend the winter months shooting a service production at a soundstage in Burnaby, and as a cautionary tale for you, the reader, here is my original screenplay for a short film dealing with actions and consequences. It's a powerful and dramatic work with a strong female lead, gritty dialogue, and an authentic *mise en scène*. Non-traditional and diverse casting for principal roles is encouraged. Qualified for Canada Media Fund and Telefilm funding. Fully tax credit eligible. Just saying.

It Never Rains but It Pours

A short film

Written by Ian Ferguson

We FADE IN *to an* ESTABLISHING SHOT *of a small café somewhere in the Lower Mainland, the sort of place that seems both timeless and anachronistic in look. We could be in almost any era since the 1930s, and only the quick glimpse of passing hybrid cars and elastane-adorned cyclists gives us a hint of the time and place. The flickering neon sign reads: "Sunny Break Eats." It is raining.*

CUT TO *the interior of the* SUNNY BREAK EATS, *a small homely and yet homey joint, the type of business that was never designed or planned out, but has evolved over time into not just a restaurant but the main gathering place for the neighbourhood. There are a handful of mismatched tables that look out over the glistening reflections of brake lights and fluorescent safety tape on the rainy sidewalk, and a small counter with a number of stools that partition off the public area of the café from the kitchen. The walls are freshly painted and the artwork that would normally be hanging on them is placed carefully on the drop cloths. There is a bulletin board by the front door that has layers of notices and flyers pinned to it. A handwritten sign reads "We serve breakfast all day every day."*

DARLA JEAN *is behind the counter and, based on her business-like demeanour and efficient movements, more than just a waitress. She is the proprietor of the establishment and in almost constant motion as she wipes the counter, stacks dishes in the bus pan, fills salt and pepper shakers, and uses an olive fork to remove baby gherkins from a jar. She does everything in a brisk manner despite the complete lack of customers in the café.*

We HEAR *the sound of a bell as the front door to the café opens, and* DARLA JEAN *looks up and pauses in her work.* HERBIE TAYLOR *enters, removing his oilskin slicker, which he shakes off and hangs on a heavy wooden coat hanger by the front door. The coat rack is made of a single piece of thick wood with what appear to be railroad spikes driven into it to hold jackets. It's that kind of a place.* HERBIE TAYLOR *is in his 50s and comfortably overweight.*

HERBIE TAYLOR crosses to the counter and sits. DARLA JEAN *has a cup of coffee in front of him on the countertop the moment he sits down. She slides a creamer over to* HERBIE TAYLOR; *he puts a dollop of cream in his cup and then carefully pours a small amount of sugar onto his coffee spoon, slowly pours it into his coffee, and then stirs it once. He takes a sip, shakes his head, and fills his spoon with another infinitesimal amount of sugar, stirs it, tastes it, and grimaces. He pours sugar directly into his coffee. It's a lot.*

DARLA JEAN

You're supposed to be cutting back.

HERBIE TAYLOR

How can a man enjoy his morning coffee
without a healthy amount of sugar in it?

DARLA JEAN

Or an unhealthy amount, eh? You'd better not let
your wife catch you. You know how she worries
about your diabetes.

HERBIE TAYLOR

I don't have diabetes. I'm just fat.

DARLA JEAN

Well, that too.

HERBIE TAYLOR

It's kind of rainy today, eh?

DARLA JEAN

Yes. Yes, it is.

HERBIE TAYLOR

Rainy tomorrow too, I reckon . . .

DARLA JEAN *sighs audibly as she pours* **HERBIE TAYLOR** *a
refill. This time he doesn't go through the ritual of mea-
suring the sugar. He just pours in a good amount, stirs his
cup, takes a swig, and smacks his lips.*

DARLA JEAN

I suppose.

HERBIE TAYLOR

Gonna rain all week, maybe . . .

73

DARLA JEAN

Honestly? We're in a rainforest. We're on the coast.
It's the rainy season. Of course it's going to rain.
Honestly.

HERBIE TAYLOR

Well, you don't have to bite my head off about it.

DARLA JEAN

It would be nice, just nice, if once you would come in here and talk about something besides the weather. That would be nice. Honestly.

There's just a bit of an awkward pause. HERBIE TAYLOR *is a little taken aback, but he's not the type of fellow to be put off for long. He holds up his cup for yet another refill, and as* DARLA JEAN *pours him his third cup of coffee . . .*

HERBIE TAYLOR

Say, Darla? Darla Jean?

DARLA JEAN

Yes, Herbie?

HERBIE TAYLOR

Say . . . how's business?

This question stops DARLA JEAN *in her tracks, and she pauses for the first time since we've seen her.* HERBIE TAYLOR *fills his cup with sugar and stirs.*

DARLA JEAN

Well, thank you for asking. Honestly. Actually . . . business could be better. Things are a little slow right now.

HERBIE TAYLOR

Not surprised.

CLOSE-UP *on* HERBIE TAYLOR *as he takes a deep, satisfying swig of his coffee.*

HERBIE TAYLOR
With the rain and all . . .

CLOSE-UP *on* DARLA JEAN *as she* REACTS. *We* HEAR *the bell over the door ring again, and* BERNIE L'ONDÉE *enters, shaking off his rain jacket and hanging it next to* HERBIE TAYLOR'S *coat. Nobody seems to use umbrellas.* BERNIE L'ONDÉE *is 35 years old, remarkably handsome, possibly a bit dim, and obviously smitten with* DARLA JEAN. *He sits at the counter next to* HERBIE TAYLOR.

BERNIE L'ONDÉE
(*To* HERBIE TAYLOR) Herbie . . .

HERBIE TAYLOR
(*To* BERNIE L'ONDÉE) Youngster . . . how goes it?

BERNIE L'ONDÉE
(*To* HERBIE TAYLOR) Can't complain—

HERBIE TAYLOR
(*To* BERNIE L'ONDÉE, cutting him off)—And nobody would listen if you did.

BERNIE L'ONDÉE
(*To* HERBIE TAYLOR) Huh? (*To* DARLA JEAN) Hey there, Darla Jean . . .

DARLA JEAN
Bernie.

75

BERNIE L'ONDÉE
Could I trouble you for a cup of coffee?

DARLA JEAN
No trouble at all.

As DARLA JEAN *turns away to get a cup from the service counter,* HERBIE TAYLOR *elbows* BERNIE L'ONDÉE. *It's a silent message being passed from the older, married man to the younger, single man. The message is "talk to her, for crying out loud." And* BERNIE L'ONDÉE's *puzzled reaction gets a silent "you dummy" response from* HERBIE TAYLOR. *The cup of coffee is placed in front of* BERNIE L'ONDÉE, *he considers it, and picks it up with both hands to take a sip. No cream or sugar for him.*

BERNIE L'ONDÉE

(*Attempting to make small talk to* DARLA JEAN) You're painting the place pink, eh?

DARLA JEAN

Does it look pink to you?

BERNIE L'ONDÉE

(*Afraid this might be a trick question*) Well ... yeah.

HERBIE TAYLOR

I also think it looks pink.

DARLA JEAN

It's not supposed to look pink.

HERBIE TAYLOR

It's not?

BERNIE L'ONDÉE

Really?

DARLA JEAN

This (*she indicates the freshly painted wall*) is supposed to be salmon.

HERBIE TAYLOR

(*Carefully*) So, it's not coloured pink it's actually
salmon-coloured.

DARLA JEAN

Correct.

BERNIE L'ONDÉE

Except it isn't.

DARLA JEAN

Isn't what?

BERNIE L'ONDÉE

It's not salmon-coloured. Salmon are shiny
and sort of silvery coloured.

DARLA JEAN

Not on the inside. When you cook a salmon
(*Indicates wall*) that's what they look like.
That's the colour.

CLOSE-UP *on* BERNIE L'ONDÉE *as he* REACTS.

BERNIE L'ONDÉE

Yeah, but then we're all sort of salmon-coloured,
aren't we? You know, on the inside?

There is an awkward pause. HERBIE TAYLOR *elbows* BERNIE
L'ONDÉE *again. This time the message gets through loud
and clear.* BERNIE L'ONDÉE, *takes a sip of his coffee to for-
tify himself, draws a deep breath, and attempts, once
again, to make conversation.*

77

BERNIE L'ONDÉE

(*To* DARLA JEAN) So ... how's business?

HERBIE TAYLOR

(*To* BERNIE L'ONDÉE) I was just asking.

(*To* DARLA JEAN) Wasn't I just?

DARLA JEAN

(*To* BERNIE L'ONDÉE) Business has been a little slow.

BERNIE L'ONDÉE

Oh, that's too bad.

It's probably on account of all the rain.

CLOSE-UP *on* DARLA JEAN *as she* REACTS. *Then* ON *the two men as* HERBIE TAYLOR *gives* BERNIE L'ONDÉE *a disappointed look.* DARLA JEAN *stabs* BERNIE L'ONDÉE *in the eye with the olive fork. He collapses to the floor, writhing in pain. The camera* PULLS OUT *and we watch as* DARLA JEAN *returns to tidying the lunch counter.* HERBIE TAYLOR *takes a careful sip of coffee.* BEAT.

HERBIE TAYLOR

Well, he had it coming.

FADE TO BLACK

ROLL CREDITS

FINIS

6 Food and Stuff

SURVIVING THE CUISINE

Salmon. So much salmon. British Columbians are inordinately proud of their salmon. The moment you arrive you will be offered salmon. Raw salmon, baked salmon, broiled salmon, basted salmon, coddled salmon, and, only rarely, fried salmon, because cholesterol. It's the equivalent of being "screeched in" in Newfoundland, except on the other coast of Canada you only have to kiss the cod; you're not forced to consume it at every single meal.

I must now confess that I have a deep and abiding antipathy to salmon. This lifelong aversion comes from growing up in northern Alberta, where mos t of the fish we consumed was of the tinned variety. Oh, you could yank a walleye out of the Peace River in the summertime, but without refrigeration, let alone electricity, if you were going eat seafood in the wintertime it came in a can. Although smoked jackfish or "fish jerky" was available.[1] Canned tuna was okay, canned sardines were palatable, but the salmon? Once the can opener had done its job, what was revealed was a greyish, pinkish chunk of slimy gelatinous flesh with just a bit of an unpleasant odour.

79

---

1   Imagine shoe leather that smelled like cat food. Yum. Good eating.

Oh, and a bone in the centre. So we weren't buying the deluxe brands.

I have tried, over the years, to educate my palate. I've ordered salmon in restaurants, consumed it at literary events, and even, once, cooked it my own self in my own kitchen. None of this changed my opinion. If anything, these attempts to educate my palate resulted in a hardening of my attitude. And possibly my arteries.

I put this down to regional disadvantages and geographical impediments. Why eat salmon in Saskatoon or Winnipeg or even Toronto? It doesn't come from those places. It's like ordering lobster in Calgary. Stick to the beef. It's local. And the locals know how to cook it properly. Here's a good rule of thumb: If your entrée had to change planes on the flight before it arrived on your supper table, you shouldn't expect it to be an epicurean delight.

So I was absolutely thrilled when a friend of mine returned from a fishing trip to Haida Gwaii and invited me and a few other pals over to enjoy a salmon he'd caught that very morning. Fish so fresh a good veterinarian could've saved its life. Perfectly grilled over charcoal with the lightest of maple syrup glazes, served on a bed of locally grown pesticide-free greens, it was proclaimed by all and sundry to be the finest meal of salmon they'd ever enjoyed. Every single person raved about how good that salmon tasted. Me? Meh. I mean, it was okay, I guess, but I obviously have no taste for salmon and I'm apparently not going to develop one.

You, however, should prepare yourself. You will have to chow down on Chinook salmon, scoff Sockeye salmon, and chew Coho salmon. Here's a helpful hint: They all taste exactly the same. Not that you'll ever catch a local admitting to this. They will all claim they can tell the difference. They are all lying. But then, as I've established, I don't much care for salmon. So it could just be me.² What I'm trying to say is, given the opportunity, switch to the halibut, which at least is usually breaded and deep-fried.

Luckily there is more to British Columbia cuisine than salmon. As noted in Chapter Three, BC is the most ethnically diverse province in Canada. This multiculturalism extends to the food available. You can eat Indian, Japanese, Chinese, Vietnamese, Korean, and Thai food in any city. Even Kamloops. And at a broad range of prices. You want expensive bánh mì? Cheap gaeng daeng? Take-out tonkatsu? You can choose to spend as little or as much as you want. There are a plethora of possibilities, although there is a paucity of Welsh restaurants in the province, the locals not having developed a taste for glamorgan or cawl.

The good news is that most of the food and drink you consume in British Columbia won't kill you. Although some of the celebrity chefs might. "You don't think there's enough salmon in your salmon smoothie? Die, diner, die!" Don't be concerned if this is said by a chef of German extraction; it just means "the dinner, the." Chefs are usually high-strung and will often repeat themselves.

Some of the more famous chefs to hail from BC include Vikram Vij, Etsuko Needham, Rob Feenie, Tabatha Stahl, and Hidekazu Tojo. The odds of having one of them actually cook your meal are slim, however. They're all too busy writing cookbooks and appearing on television. I'm only mentioning them in an attempt to weasel a free meal. And to point out that high-end restaurants are available for your dining pleasure.

Most of these joints will have names like Orü, Glö, Füd, and, I guess, Ümlaüt. You can easily drop a bundle on a world-class meal lovingly prepared with the best of local ingredients

---

2   It's not just me; all salmon tastes the same.

in an internationally renowned kitchen as you relax and enjoy the atmosphere and ambience. If you like that sort of thing.

Let's be honest, though, most of us don't eat at these type of places. Not on a regular basis. It costs too much and, even if you can afford to eat every meal at Tojo's or Vij's, you probably shouldn't. Part of the appeal of fine dining is the special occasion aspect of the experience. If you do dine in one of the posh places, remember what we covered in Chapter Four. Don't dress up. You'll stand out like a sore thumb.

You will be pleased to learn that many of the same chain restaurants you frequent back home, wherever home is, also have locations in British Columbia. However, if you want to eat like a local British Columbian, you should know that there are also chains that started right here in BC and even some that are unique to the province. I'm not including any chains that have come and gone. What would be the point, really, if you can't eat at them?[3] Here then, in chronological order, newest to oldest, are British Columbia's contributions to the world of franchised restaurant brands:

1) **Brown's Social House:** established in 2004 in North Vancouver. Upscale casual dining restaurant with 30 locations, mainly in Western Canada.

2) **Memphis Blues BBQ House:** established in 2001 in Vancouver. Barbecue restaurant with a dozen locations in BC and Alberta.

3) **Cactus Club:** established in 1988 in North Vancouver. Upscale casual dining restaurant with 27 locations, mainly in Western Canada.

---

3   The Aristocratic, the Silk Hat, Henri's Grill & Smorgasbord, all long gone, but not forgotten. Well, actually ... forgotten.

4) Panago: established in 1986 in Abbotsford. Takeout and delivery pizza restaurant with 200 locations across Canada.

5) Vera's Burger Shack: established in 1977 in West Vancouver. Gourmet burger restaurant with 17 locations across Canada.

6) The Pantry: established in 1975 in Abbotsford. Family restaurant with 6 locations in BC, and 1 in Alberta.

7) Romeo's Pizza: established in 1974 in Victoria. Italian restaurant with 5 locations in BC, all on Vancouver Island.

8) The Keg (originally Keg'n Cleaver): established in 1971 in North Vancouver. Steak house restaurant with 160 locations across Canada and the United States.

9) Ricky's All-Day Grill (originally Ricky's Pancake House): established in 1962 in West Vancouver. Family restaurant with 67 locations across Canada.

Canada's oldest and longest-running restaurant chain comes from BC. White Spot was established way back in 1928 in Vancouver. They have locations world-wide, including Hong Kong and Seoul. They are famous, or perhaps notorious, for their special Triple "O" hamburger sauce. The secret ingredients are relish and mayonnaise. I know, I know. You can also order from White Spot on BC Ferries. So, if you're taking a voyage across the skookumchuck, at least you won't have to make a special trip to pick up a Pirate Pack[4] for the kids.

If you've eaten in a Cactus Club and a Brown's Social House, you'd be forgiven for assuming they are the exact same

83

---

4   Or Pirate Pak. I've spotted it spelled both ways.

restaurant. And that restaurant would be an Earl's. Or maybe a Moxie's. There's not a lot to differentiate the two, but you can get a slice of key lime pie at the Cactus Club, courtesy of rocker Tal Bachman, who convinced Chef Rob Feenie to keep it on the menu.

Memphis Blues continues the long-standing tradition of Canadian restaurant chains using US names: Boston Pizza, New York Fries, Montana's, East Side Mario's, etc. All 100% Canadian. This isn't, I've noticed, reciprocal. When I travel in the USA, I don't get to stop in for a bite at Saskatchewan Smith's Sausage Shop or the East of Edson Eatery. So much for the North American Free Trade Agreement, eh? The brand spankin' new United States-Mexico-Canada Agreement[5] hasn't been any more helpful. Although I have come up with a good concept for a south-of-the-border chain of restaurants: Priscilla's Prairie Perogy Parlour. The superfluous Canadian "U" in "parlour" is part of the branding. Also all alliteration. Contact me for franchise information.

You'll notice that North Vancouver and West Vancouver account for half (or 50% in metric) of the list. I can only assume the quality of the local cuisine was so poor in those locations it drove people to start their own restaurants. Talk about yer founder's syndrome.

British Columbia has the highest percentage of vegetarians in the country, so you should prepare yourself for meals consisting of kale, quinoa, and tofu. If you end up eating in a vegan restaurant, or even worse, eating with (shudder) actual vegans, be prepared for a meal consisting of chickpeas, lawn clippings, and sanctimony. What's the difference between a vegetarian and a vegan, you ask? Don't worry, both groups will instantly identify themselves and explain. And lecture. Vegans will also hector, browbeat, and badger. They will

---

5   USMCA, which also stands for Underhanded Sneaky Mendacious Continental Agreement.

also refer to Patriarchal Food Culture and Misogynistic Meat Logic, so you might not want to mention that cheeseburger you had at Vera's Burger Shack. Basically, vegetarians are annoying and vegans are insufferable.

British Columbians pride themselves on eating locally sourced food, even if that food is often sourced from their local Whole Foods Market or Thrifty's. They also like local beer. The first craft brew pub in Canada, and the first in all of North America, opened up in 1982. And almost immediately went broke. Two years later, Spinnakers opened up and is still going strong, relegating the Horseshoe Bay Brewery to the Pete Best section of microbrewery history.

BC is now home to countless small independent microbreweries and brew pubs offering beers and ales under brand names such as Anarchist Alligator and Helmetless Bicyclist. They all taste the same. Like the salmon.[6] Although a BC beer connoisseur would beg to differ. For me, an IPA is an IPA, a stout is a stout, and a pale ale is a pale ale, no matter what name they go by.

Speaking of pale ale, you should know that you can no longer purchase Albino Rhino Pale Ale, despite this being a popular brand for over twenty-five years. There was a complaint about the name being offensive. No, I'm not kidding. The beer was, of course, named after a breed of rhinoceros, the albino rhinoceros to be precise, also known as the white rhinoceros or square-lipped rhinoceros but, alas, the beer is now extinct and the rhino isn't doing much better.

This is what you've got to be wary of when you go out for a drink in British Columbia. For every beer lover who

---

6 The way Wild Salmon is often actually Farmed Salmon, your Craft Beer is more than likely produced by one of the Big Breweries. If you happen to be a beer snob, I'm sorry to break the news, but your pint of Mom & Pop's Killarney Flimflammer is probably made by the same international conglomerate that makes Labatt's or Coors or Teflon. Often with the same ingredients.

will gently chide you for ordering a Molson's Canadian, there will also be a beer bully who will angrily attack your choice of libation as a microbrew microaggression. They might even bring up climate change or pipelines or even the Canucks penalty kill as part of their argument. Best to avoid ordering your usual. The "Non-discriminatory North Shore Amber Ale" is usually a safe, politically correct choice.

You should, given the opportunity, check out some of the First Nations restaurants available in the province and tuck into some bannock, Indian tacos, buffalo burgers, or even, if you must, wild smoked salmon. I know what you're thinking. Surely the correct name is Native North American Aboriginal First Nations Indigenous Peoples Tacos? I called my sister to check. "Nope," she said, "we're still calling them Indian Tacos." She went on to add, "I wish White People would lighten up." My favourites are the Salmon & Bannock Bistro in Vancouver (despite the name), the Lelem' Café in Fort Langley, and the Kekuli Café in Merritt, which just opened a second location in the Okanagan, meaning they are on their way to joining Brown's Social House and White Spot on the list of BC-born chains.

You should also know how to spot a spot prawn. Only available in British Columbia, this local delicacy can be enjoyed during May to June. The best way to get them is to buy them right off the boat. Go to False Creek, or Steveston, or any Fisherman's Wharf (a common subtitle in BC) and enjoy the most succulent of crustaceans. Unless, of course, you have a shellfish allergy, in which case you'll not only want to avoid the wharfs, you should also stay away from any restaurant that serves seafood until the season ends. Panago would be a safe bet.

If you're a fan of sushi and you've ever eaten a California roll (crab, avocado, cucumber, and all the fixings), you should know that it was invented in British Columbia by Chef Hidekazu

Tojo. Maybe. There's a bit of controversy over the origins, but he absolutely did invent the BC roll. What's in a BC roll? Salmon. Always with the salmon.

And for dessert, you'll want to try a Nanaimo bar. What's in a Nanaimo bar? The usual answer is "bikers and strippers," but it's actually custard, coconut, cocoa, and chocolate. The four "C's" of contentment. The bar was invented, again maybe, by the Women's Hospital Auxiliary Association of the Nanaimo Hospital, in, natch, Nanaimo. Hence the name. It probably predates its first cookbook appearance back in 1952, but it is a gift British Columbia has given to the world. Canada Post recently released a postage stamp celebrating the Nanaimo bar. Didn't look anything like the real deal. Too much custard and not enough base.[7] Still, it's the thought that counts.

According to most people the three most beautiful words in the English language are "I love you." Although some would say the three most beautiful words in the English language are "enclosed find cheque." With direct deposit and e-transfers and, I suppose, bitcoin and such, nobody's really writing cheques any more. Myself, I believe the three most beautiful words in the English language are "All Day Breakfast."[8]

If you're like me and you enjoy a good breakfast, at, say, any hour of the day or night, well, you got off the elevator on the right floor.

British Columbia is the best province in all of Canada for diners. You got your chain diners, your retro diners, your refurbished diners, even your hipster diners. There's a trend in BC of hipsters taking over original, long-standing diners and upgrading the menu and service. It's like saving the façade on a heritage building while gutting the interior. Sure

87

---

7   Sort of like the BC Conservatives.
8   The five most beautiful words in the English language are: All You Can Eat Buffet.

it may be an improvement, but it still feels a little depressing. If you go online and look up "diner nearest me" you'll be astonished at the variety of options available. Here's a helpful hint: If the word "diner" is in the name of the restaurant, it's probably run by hipsters. Not that you won't enjoy your salmon Benedict, but you'll be dropping $18.90. And they'll charge for refills.

I'm partial to authentic diners. What do I mean by authentic, you ask? I mean the sort of place kitted out with faded battleship linoleum on the floor, mismatching tables laminated in melamine, leatherette booths patched with duct tape, and, if possible, a lunch counter with stools offering nothing in the way of lower-back support. The kind of joint that's been around for a while and is—let's be honest—just a little on the tatty side. Cheap eats, in other words; a place where you can tuck into pancakes and eggs at 3:00 o'clock in the afternoon (or 3:00 o'clock in the morning, depending on hours of operation and your personal schedule), gulp back endless cups of coffee from a bottomless pot, and still get change back from a Viola Desmond (in metric: a ten dollar bill) when you settle up.

I'm talking about the sort of real-deal dining experience you won't discover online. The sort of place that doesn't have a website or any reviews on Tripadvisor, let alone Yelp. The kind of place that Skip the Dishes delivery drivers skip. What could, if one were being uncharitable, be described as a greasy spoon, but is better considered to be the inspiration for the Sunny Break Eats in my screenplay from the previous chapter.

Here, as a service to you, the reader, is my completely unscientific and purely alphabetical list of genuine article bona fide diners. I've eaten in 'em all, and they not only serve up good grub, they also serve as a good way to judge people. If I meet someone who, say, doesn't like dogs, then I don't like

them. Says something about their character. If I invite someone for a meal at one of the places below and they don't like
it? Same thing. In my opinion, these are the best diners in BC:

1) Alice's Restaurant, Nanaimo.

2) Fresgo Inn Restaurant, Surrey.

3) Helen's Grill, Vancouver.

4) KC's Café, Port Coquitlam. Bring cash; they don't take
   credit cards or debit.

5) Marble Arch, Saanich. Also cash only.

6) Red Kettle Restaurant, Victoria.

Honourable mention to:

7) John's Place, Victoria. Too well-known to make the
   official list above.

8) Molly's Reach, Gibsons. Because *The Beachcombers*.

9) Northern Star Café, Smithers. Technically a Chinese
   buffet.

No, I'm not angling for a free meal from any of them. Their
prices are already low enough. Tell them I sent you, though.
They may stare blankly at you if you drop my name, but if
you describe me as "the old guy who reads all the newspa-
pers," they'll know who you're talking about. Also, there's no
guarantee any of these restaurants will survive into the future
in their present unvarnished form, so don't waste time. Get
there before the rising cost of doing business, the rising small
business tax (which isn't, despite the name, small), or rising
land valuations close their doors for good. Or before risible
hipsters eagerly gentrify them into some sort of conceptual

postmodern diner. The genuine article is an endangered species. Like the albino rhinoceros and the daily newspaper. Enjoy it before it goes away forever.

Now let us compare coffee. And culture. Or coffee culture if you will. In the rest of Canada, folks are often divided thusly: Tim Hortons or Starbucks. Smartphone App or Roll Up the Rim. Coffee that tastes burnt versus watery coffee. You know, the existential differences that make up the warp and weft of the very fabric of society. British Columbians, as always, march to the beat of a different drummer. The province is home to more independent coffee shops, coffee roasters, coffee importers, coffee brands, and possibly coffee sommeliers than the rest of the country combined.

As a newcomer to BC, you'll not only have to quickly learn a dozen different ways to order your coffee (if your regular order is a "non-fat decaf extra-foam latte with a gluten-free spelt muffin," you can shorten it to "Gimme a why-bother") but you will also have to learn the difference between Blenz, Moka House, Habit, Caffè Artigiano, and Murchie's, not to mention the dozens of other small local chains, let alone the literally hundreds of standalone coffee shops. Here's a hint: Murchie's is a tea house.

Starbucks didn't open its first non-US store in British Columbia way back in 1987 to develop a market; there was already one here. The Baristas of British Columbia[9] regularly compete in national and international coffee-making competitions and usually win. This is more than any of the professional sports teams can manage. British Columbians take their coffee as seriously as they take their politics. In both cases they want ethical fair trade served steaming hot in a reusable cup with a Bill Reid graphic on the side.

---

9   Also the title of the sequel to *The Bridges of Madison County*.

All of which is wasted on me. I view coffee strictly as a caffeine delivery service. I went to Discovery Coffee, only to discover that I couldn't tell the difference between their coffee and a cup of mud from Good Earth. They both tasted okay. Although I can't tell the difference between a good cup of coffee and a bad one, you probably can and do. If you like good coffee, you've arrived in the right place. So I've been informed. You can get a good cup of joe anywhere in the province, even Kamloops.

Now, halfway through this book, I know what you must be asking: "What's with all the lists?" Good question. The lists in this survival guide are because:

1) lists are easy to write,

2) lists give the impression of detailed research and scientific rigour where none exists,

3) you can create humour simply by repeating an item on the list, and

4) lists are easy to write.[10]

10 This is also from *How to Be a Canadian*. The ~~eagerly anticipated~~ ~~long awaited~~ absurdly overdue follow-up, *Being Canadian: Your Guide to the Best* Country in the World*, is heading to a bookstore near you.

7   Governance through Shenanigans

SURVIVING THE POLITICS

There's a non-geographical reason British Columbia is called The Left Coast. The politics here are, to say the least, different from those of the rest of the country. The way left-handed people are different from the rest of the population. Nothing sinister about it, most of the time, although the folks in charge, both provincially and municipally, often feel by dint of being elected (or occasionally scamming their way into office) that they have been given a mandate for magical thinking and shenanigans.

It was tempting to make this the shortest section in the book. The chapter title could have been "How the Province of British Columbia is Governed," the first sentence would read "It isn't," and, boom, that's all, folks. Time to turn the page and learn all about cultural pursuits and other less complicated subjects.[1]

However, being as this is a survival guide and all, it seemed irresponsible to not give you at least a basic understanding of the dysfunctional politics of BC. You've got your right-wing nut bars in the Interior and your left-wing flakes on the coast, creating a nutty, flaky granola bar of civic engagement. Or at least noise. Both groups tend to shout an awful lot.

---

1   From *How to Be a Canadian*, Chapter 14: "How the Canadian Government Works. It Doesn't." That's the entire chapter. Did I mention the sequel is finally finished?

This is part of the history and culture of the province. It
goes right back to the very beginning when Captain James
Cook discovered what is now Vancouver Island in 1778. This
"discovery" came as a surprise to the First Nations who
were already living here. All of a sudden trading posts and
forts were springing up in traditional territories that had
been occupied for over three thousand years. Bit unnerv-
ing, that. And the province never got around to signing any
treaties with the Indigenous population, leaving the legal
question of who actually, you know, owns the place unre-
solved until ... Well, they're still working on it today. And
by "working on it," I mean ignoring it and hoping the issue
eventually goes away.

What the rest of the country refers to as "Crown land"
is, in British Columbia, "unceded territory," meaning title
to the land was never surrendered by the Indigenous population or acquired by the government. The vast majority of
the province is unceded,[2] which has given rise to the "land
acknowledgement," a spoken statement before public gather-
ings and political meetings.

I had never encountered this before moving to British
Columbia. I was asked to join the Film Commission, and after
all the introductions and handshakes and, apparently, really
good coffee,[3] the first meeting opened with the chair reading
the following:

> "We acknowledge that we are gathered on the
> unceded territory of the Lekwungen people."

"Kind of neat" was my thought. Then it was onto the business of approving the minutes from the previous meeting

---

2   First Nations territorial claims add up to 115% of the total land mass of British
Columbia, so they're probably including that bit that Alaska stole.
3   Like I would know.

and sitting though self-serving and mildly vainglorious state-
ments disguised as motions. You know, the usual committee
stuff. When we took a break, I asked a fellow board member
about the speech that began the evening.

"Well," he said, "it's the least we can do."

"Yeah, quite literally," I said, foreshadowing why I only
served one term.[4]

The land acknowledgement started in British Columbia
but has since spread across the country, although in other
provinces it refers to traditional territories, as opposed to
unceded, since those other governments stole the land and
screwed over the First Nations already living there all nice
and legal like.

British Columbia joined Confederation in 1871. They did
so because they owed money. They were broke, despite the
fur trade and the gold rush. They cut a deal to get the rest of
Canada to pay off the massive debt they'd run up, and also,
hey, while you're at it, we'd like a transcontinental railroad
built through the mountains. How hard could that be? I mean,
unless you want us to all become Americans, eh?

British Columbia basically came into being as a con job.
This has laid the foundation for much of what has happened
since. This chapter will get you up to speed with the many
scandals, hustles, and indictable offences that helped build
the province.

Let's begin with Provincial Shenanigans.

Politics is a blood sport in other provinces. Ontario, say,
or even New Brunswick. In Quebec, it's *plutôt un abattoir de
mauvais sentiments*. Alberta? Maybe a tractor pull. In British
Columbia, provincial politics could best be described as a
compost bin. You know, that green plastic thingy with the

---

4 And using "literally" correctly.

perforated lid. With the theoretically biodegradable bag liner that bursts and leaks the moment you toss in the first banana peel. In other words, provincial politics in British Columbia is messy and smelly and doesn't deliver what it promises.

In British Columbia, the Liberals are Conservatives, the Conservatives are non-existent, the NDP are in power, and the Green Party are in charge. The big tent party, the discontent party, the tent city party, and the big hemp party. In BC, it's not so much "Good Government" as it is "Good Grief."

The capital city is Victoria. It was originally supposed to be in New Westminster. At the deciding debate a drunken Member of the Legislative Assembly, one William Franklyn, speaking in support of New West, caused such hilarity with his attempts to sway the vote he cost New Westminster the opportunity to be the seat of government.

There have been thirty-six premiers of British Columbia since the province first signed onto the articles of Confederation. Some of the more notable ones to hold that office are:

John Foster McCreight—served 1871 to 1872. The first premier of British Columbia. Hooray! He was heading for Australia when he made a wrong turn and ended up in what was then the Colony of Vancouver Island. Described as bad tempered, obstinate, and utterly ignorant of politics by his contemporaries, he set the standard for those who followed.

Amor De Cosmos—served 1872 to 1874. Born William Smith, British Columbia's second premier changed his name to what he claimed was Latin for "lover of the universe," despite having a "volatile temperament." He founded the *Daily British Colonist* newspaper, now the *Times-Colonist*, before going into politics and hustled the federal government to build the railroad and provide "monetary guarantees," which forced his resignation from provincial politics. He ended up in Ottawa as an MP and was an opponent of territorial concessions for the First Nations in BC, which makes him responsible for today's land acknowledgements. Known contemporaneously as, duh, "an eccentric," British Columbia's Father of Confederation was declared insane in 1895.

Joseph Martin—served 1900 to 1900. The 13th premier of British Columbia, for you triskaidekaphobians, lasted all of three months in the job. He was also described by folks at the time as being "quick to umbrage" and "unsuited to political office." You may be noticing a pattern.

James Dunsmuir—served 1900 to 1902. BC's 14th premier was the first to encourage Chinese immigration. Yay! Oh, but not for humanitarian reasons. He wanted cheap labour for the coal mines and railroads.

Harlan Carey Brewster—served 1916 to 1918. The 18th premier instituted prohibition in British Columbia. He appointed Walter Findlay as Prohibition Commissioner. Findlay was a bootlegger. Not the most obvious choice. Walter Findlay was arrested less than a year into his first term for "illegal import of liquor" as well as breach of trust. He was convicted, served two years, and got out just when prohibition was repealed in 1920.

John Oliver—served 1918 to 1927. The 19th premier of British Columbia. Now hosts a talk show.

Simon Fraser Tolmie—served 1928 to 1933. The 21st premier, and last Conservative to be elected, was defeated when he attempted to cut government benefits and social services. I'm just saying.

Boss Johnson—served 1947 to 1952. The 24th premier, best known as the bad guy on *Dukes of Hazzard*.

W.A.C. Bennett—served 1952 to 1972. The 25th premier of British Columbia, and the longest-serving one, also called "Wacky" Bennett, known for building highways, railways, ferries, and dams, and naming most of them after himself. Also created ICBC, so grrr ... Was in power so long the voters decided to elect the NDP.

Dave Barrett—served 1972 to 1975. The 26th premier began the tradition of the NDP taking over for brief periods of time due to voter fatigue and outrage with the sitting government.

Bill Bennett—served 1975 to 1986. The son also rises. The voters, having flirted with the NDP, returned the Social Credit Party to power. They went on to win three elections in a row and were surely going to be the natural governing party of British Columbia in perpetuity. What could go wrong?

Bill Vander Zalm—served 1986 to 1991. Oh, right. This guy. Bill Bennett tossed him the keys and Bill Vander Zalm drove the car off the cliff. Resigned in disgrace over conflict of interest allegations regarding Fantasyland, a theme park he owned. Not kidding. Was subsequently acquitted at trial, although the presiding judge said he had behaved in a manner that

was "foolish and ill-advised and in breach of ethics."
John Foster McCreight would be so proud.

The NDP won the subsequent election and even the one
after that. They were in power from 1991 to 2001. Who was the
premier during that time? Glad you asked. First up was Mike
Harcourt. He resigned in disgrace as a result of "Bingogate."
Followed by Glen Clark. He resigned in disgrace because
of "Casinogate." Dan Miller became interim leader of the
party and, for a brief time, premier. He resigned from
the party before the next election.[5] Ujjal Dosanjh took over
for one year before leading the party to defeat in 2001.[6]

Gordon Campbell became the 34th premier of British
Columbia. The Liberal party were in power for the first
time. They won the next five elections. Not all of them with
Gordon Campbell at the helm. He resigned in disgrace
in 2011 because of "Railgate." Or maybe because of that
time the RCMP raided the BC Legislature, or because he
brought in the HST after campaigning against it, or maybe
it was because he got busted for drunk driving in Hawaii.
Whatever. Doesn't matter.

Christy Clark then became the first female premier of
British Columbia. Yee and/or Haw! She won the 2013 election
and the 2017 election. So, why isn't she around, you may ask?
Did she resign in disgrace? Nope. What happened was in the
last election Christy Clark's Liberal Party won a minority of
seats and the NDP and the Green Party, quickly counting on
their fingers, realized if they combined their seats they would
be tied with the Liberals, and—once the Speaker of the House
was appointed—they could take over.

98

---

5   Not in disgrace. Dan Miller always marched to the beat of a different drummer.
6   Which was disgraceful, but at least he was defeated before he, oh, I don't know,
resigned in disgrace or something.

Finally, after six years of a woman running the province, middle-aged white guys were back in charge. Phew!

And those middle-aged white guys would be: John Horgan, the 36th and current premier of British Columbia, and his consigliore Andrew Weaver, the current leader of the Greens. As far as policy is concerned, the parties don't have a lot in common. And the two leaders can't stand each other. It's like a pilot episode for a sitcom about roommates: "This week on *Grin and Bear It* Andy tries to get John to turn down the thermostat; John needs Andy's help to stop anonymous voting."

The last part is true, by the way. The NDP wanted to pass a law allowing unions to use a show of hands rather than secret ballot when seeking certification. Andrew Weaver said no. Not part of the deal he made when they brought down the Liberals and made John Horgan the premier.

What *was* part of the deal was holding a referendum on electoral reform. Under our current first-past-the-post system or FPTP (pronounced "fhhtpt"), a candidate doesn't need an outright majority of votes to win their riding; they just need to win the most votes among competing candidates. This can lead to smaller parties, like the Greens, being underrepresented. This is why they want to reform our voting system. And it was one of the conditions of their deal with the NDP.

Now, I'm not big on proportional representation, or PR (pronounced "purr"), which is the preferred alternative to FPTP. Oh, it seems simple enough on the surface. A party that gets 12% of the vote gets 12% of the seats; a party that gets 39% of the vote gets 39% of the seats. And so on. However, half the population of BC lives in the Metro Vancouver area, and I'd bet you a salmon supper they have different priorities from the voters in the Interior or the Okanagan or even Victoria. Also, they give the Stanley Cup to the team that wins the most games, not the team that scores the most goals.

It's a moot point, though. FPTP defeated PR in the latest referendum by a greater margin than the previous referendum in 2009 or the original referendum in 2005. Yep, just like separatists in Quebec, proponents of PR keep coming back plebiscite after plebiscite, knowing they only have to win once to make it all worthwhile. And, also like separatists, they favour ridiculously complicated ballot questions.

Let me make a Swiftian "modest proposal" to everyone who feels our current system of electing politicians is unfair or somehow undemocratic. Maybe the NDP had it right regarding union certification. The solution might be to do away with secret ballots. People vote the wrong way when they aren't held accountable. Let's put scrutineers *inside* the voting booth. Then, depending on how you voted, you'd get some sort of sticker placed on your forehead[7] that would tell all and sundry which candidate you cast your ballot for. This might not change the actual results but at least you'd know who to blame. And who to publically shame.

For your own safety, don't bring up anything or anybody I've mentioned so far in conversation with any British Columbian. If you get asked about provincial politics, explain that you are a newcomer and that you couldn't possibly have an opinion one way or the other. Do not, however, use the expression "I don't have a horse in that race." Horses are a touchy subject in BC.

Also, no matter who the electorate choose, the economy of British Columbia continues to hum along and is the strongest in Canada. You should bring this up when talking to a local. Just don't mention that this is as a result of money laundering. Just because something is true, doesn't mean it isn't hurtful.

---

7   Or a scarlet letter.

Let's move on to Municipal Shenanigans.

If government at the provincial level is a sitcom, local governments are, to apply the same metaphor (or is it a simile?), more of a game show. *Dysfunctional Family Feud*, say, or *Let's Not Make a Deal*, or even *Front Page Ethically Challenged.*[8]

According to the Community Charter of the Province of British Columbia, the law that regulates municipalities, the first duty of a local council is, and I quote, to "consider the well-being and interests of the municipality and its community." Seems pretty straightforward, no?

What are the most important things a town council or city government do? Collecting property taxes? Nope. Fixing potholes? That's not it. Parking enforcement? Not even close. How about providing for the safety and security of their residents? You'd think so, but no. The most important priorities for a municipal government in British Columbia are: 1) climate change, 2) social justice, and 3) banning fun.

In the first chapter of this book, I mentioned that Vancouver's city council voted to declare the city a "nuclear weapons free zone." Kitimat, Nanaimo, and Victoria also decided to pass similar absolutely meaningless, let alone enforceable bylaws. Enforcing it is particularly tricky for Victoria, since they are right next door to Esquimalt, home to Canada's Pacific Naval Base. The United States Navy regularly anchors aircraft carriers chock-full of nuclear weapons at CFB Esquimalt. I assume if those ships cross city limits a bylaw enforcement officer swims out from Victoria and issues them a ticket.

We're now more worried about the world coming to an end from climate change than we are about nuclear Armageddon, so Vancouver just declared a climate emergency.

---

8   At the municipal level, elections are less democratic process and more Stockholm syndrome.

So did Richmond. Well, they are below sea level. And their council is treading water. Oh, and not to be outdone, so did the Capital Regional District.

The Capital Regional District is what you think of as "Victoria." You are wrong. The city of Victoria is only one of thirteen separate municipalities that make up the Greater Victoria Area, each with their own city council and mayor. After Victoria and Esquimalt, you've got Oak Bay and a bunch of cities named Saanich: East Saanich, Central Saanich, Ham 'n' Cheese Saanich, Saanichton ... as well as the ironically named View Royal, and the biblically named cities of Colwood and Metchosin. From Matthew 22:14: "Many are Colwood, few are Metchosin."

The total population is around 300,000. So one Saskatoon or one Markham or half a Winnipeg, all of which somehow manage to survive with one mayor and one city council. You'd think the sensible thing would be to maybe combine a couple of these cities. Never bring this up. It's logical, it would save money, and it would provide more efficient delivery of services to local taxpayers. So it's not going to happen.

Municipal councils have much higher priorities than amalgamation: removing statues of controversial historical figures such as John A. Macdonald, also known as "Canada's First Prime Minister," for example. Towns and cities in BC are also big on banning things. Vancouver banned doorknobs. For social justice reasons. Seriously. A whole swack of municipalities have banned single-use plastic bags and drinking straws, and there's now a movement to ban all disposable cups, plates, and cutlery. Eventually all takeout food in British Columbia will have to be eaten by hand. This is bad news for the Ron, the Scalding Hot Soup Man restaurant chain.

Mostly what local governments want to ban is fun. Penticton banned partying. Chemainus banned street hockey. Victoria has a ban on multiple bagpipes. Again, this is true. Only one bagpiper is allowed on the street at any one time. Victoria has a ton of restrictions on buskers and street performers. Panhandlers? Not so much. Victoria is, of course, a tourist destination. Folks come from all over the world to enjoy the blossoming cherry trees, the hanging flower baskets, and the horse-drawn carriages. All of which Victoria city council wants to ban.

Here's a headline for you:

VICTORIA'S NEW MAYOR REFUSES TO SWEAR OATH TO QUEEN ELIZABETH II.

That's right. Despite being elected mayor of a city named after the Queen's great-great-grandmother in a province called "British" Columbia, the newly elected mayor decided to take a principled stand against the monarchy and everything it represents. Two years later, Prince William and his wife, Kate, the Duchess of Cambridge, made a royal visit to Victoria accompanied by Prime Minister Trudeau and his wife, Sophie. The fact that the mayor took every opportunity to swan around with Their Royal Highnesses and appear in photo ops with them (and our dreamy PM) does not mean that her original refusal to swear allegiance was less a matter of conscience and more a cynical act of virtue signalling. Oh, wait. It totally does. Carry on then.

Another headline:

NEWLY ELECTED SAANICH MAYOR CLAIMS STAFF SPYING ON HIM.

This poor bastard. He gets elected and immediately claims the municipal workers at city hall have installed spyware on his computer and are bugging his phone because they have a vendetta against him. He becomes a national laughingstock along the lines of Toronto's Rob Ford. Or the Speaker of the House that time he claimed the Clerk of the Legislative Assembly shoplifted a wood splitter. The mayor continued to make ridiculous, absurd, and unsubstantiated claims, which, and you probably saw this coming, all turned out to be substantiated. It was all true. He wasn't being paranoid; they really were out to get him.

Another headline:

NANAIMO CITY COUNCIL CALLS ON RCMP TO INVESTIGATE MAYOR.

Nanaimo City Council to every other dysfunctional city council in the province: "hold my beer." Where to begin? The time the mayor sued the council? The time the council sued the mayor? The time the mediator hired to teach the council how to get along sued them? The time the department of Justice appointed a special prosecutor? The criminal investigations? The allegations of corruption? How about the time the city's chief administrator threatened to punch out the mayor? You can't fight city hall, but apparently you can fight in city hall.

And, finally, an example of all-encompassing shenanigans, including both the provincial and the municipal ... and even a school district.

The town of Cassiar opened William Story Secondary School, a brand spanking new high school in 1992. Marching bands, speeches, I assume cake. Six months later the school was closed, torn down, and sold for parts.

Believe it or not, there is one pressing social issue that has created unanimity of policy among all the different municipal governments: urban poultry. North Vancouver, Delta, Port Coquitlam, Victoria, Surrey, Burnaby, Esquimalt, Oak Bay, New Westminster, Squamish, and Vancouver have all passed bylaws allowing backyard chicken coops in residential neighbourhoods. This is viewed as a huge victory for the Fox and Racoon lobby.

Elections BC: You voted, you got what you deserved, stop complaining.

8   Entertainment and Stuff

SURVIVING THE CULTURE

If you're an art lover or a lover of the arts—and the two can be mutually exclusive—there's a lot going on in beautiful, artistic British Columbia. BC has a rich cultural tradition and a vibrant arts scene. The kind of art that hangs on walls and that other stuff like ballet, opera, puppetry, art galleries, and museums. There's a little bit of culture for everyone, kind of like flavours of yogurt, and it is available province-wide. I will begin with the performing arts, also known as entertainment you have to leave the house for that isn't a movie.

Theatre Stuff

There are six different types of theatre companies for you to choose from in British Columbia.

1) Large regional

These are professional theatre companies. They employ full-time artistic directors and hire members of the Canadian Actors' Equity Association, and the sets, costumes, and production elements will be top-notch. Their seasons will consist of plays and musicals that were popular in the West End or on Broadway three or four seasons ago. Once in a while a Canadian play will be performed. This category includes the Arts Club Theatre in Vancouver, the Gateway Theatre in Richmond, the Chemainus Theatre Festival in Chemainus, which also offers a dinner theatre option, Theatre One in Nanaimo, and Victoria's Belfry Theatre, which offers a change of pace as far as programming is concerned, preferring to program plays that were popular in Toronto or off-Broadway three or four seasons ago.

Most common audience reaction overheard in the lobby: "Hey, the actor playing the lead role is also in that Tim Hortons commercial."

2) Small regional

These are still professional theatre companies. The artistic director may also have to teach acting classes for interested adults on the weekends. The actors may or may not be members of the Canadian Actors' Equity Association, and they also may or may not all be getting paid. The sets, costumes, and production elements may be representational or even nonexistent. The shows will often be original works, original adaptations of classic works, classic adaptations of original works, and quite often Canadian. This category includes the Firehall Theatre in Vancouver; Victoria's Intrepid Theatre, Theatre Inconnu, and Theatre Skam; and the Western Canada Theatre in, of all places, Kamloops. I know.

Most common audience reaction overheard in the lobby: "Hey, the actor playing the lead role is also a cashier at my Shoppers."

3) TYA

These are professional theatre companies that provide programming for children and families, or what used to be called "children's theatre" and is now known as Theatre for Young

Audiences or TYA.[1] There are two different approaches to presenting theatre for young audiences. There are the theatre companies who have the audience come to them for the shows, which are usually, although not always, performed indoors: the Carousel Theatre in Vancouver and Kaleidoscope Theatre in Victoria, for instance. Then there are TYA companies that take the shows to their audience through touring productions. These shows are considered a rite of passage for thespians just beginning their careers, since a TYA tour means the actors are loading the set into a van at 6:30 in the morning, driving through inclement weather (which can include anything up to and including a pestilence of frogs falling from the sky), and performing in a school gymnasium. Vancouver's Green Thumb Theatre and Hooked on Books as well as Victoria's Story Theatre would be examples; Armstrong's Caravan Farm Theatre, which is technically a commune that does shows on the side, would also fit this category.

Most common audience reaction overheard during the curtain call: "Teacher, I have to go to the bathroom."

4) Canvassed

These are theatres that present the works of William Shakespeare. Shows are performed outdoors and usually under a tent of some kind, if you're lucky. Shakespearean festivals operate during the summer months, but, as I've mentioned, it does rain, just a tad, from time to time, depending on which part of the province you're enduring, so there is a need for some sort of canvas covering. The festivals can range from fully professional joints like Vancouver's Bard on the Beach to smaller operations such as the Good Will Festival in Vernon, the Cowichan Valley Shakespeare Festival in Duncan, or the Greater Victoria Shakespeare Festival. A word of warning:

---

1   Not to be confused with T&A.

Every once in a while a director will try something shocking and actually present one of the Bard of Avon's plays in the setting and time period he intended. You should immediately get up from the blanket or yoga mat you're sitting on and leave. Nobody needs that sort of negativity.

Most common audience reaction overheard during the opening soliloquy: "Why didn't we bring bug spray?"

5) Fringe

Fringe festivals are spreading across the province faster than measles in a playground.[2] Low ticket prices, independent productions, lots of first-time writers, directors, and actors . . . These festivals function sort of like junior hockey. A lot of pros have gotten their start in a fringe theatre and some do quite well touring the international fringe festival circuit. You can attend the Vancouver, Victoria, Kelowna, or Nanaimo festivals, and a new fringe may be coming soon to a city near you. The quality of shows can vary, so be prepared. You might find the show you're watching offensive. Or dull. Or, often, both.

Most common audience reaction overheard in the lineup at the porta-potty: "Well, I've never been so offended and bored in my life!"

6) Community

These are theatres that present amateur productions. They may pay a custodian and someone to look after the office, sell tickets, and run programs off on the Gestetner, or if they've upgraded, a photocopier. Everyone else will be working for free, or, in the true meaning of the word "amateur," "for the love of." The season will usually have at least one tired old British farce with a title like *Ooh, That's Me Bum, Guv'nor!* and will often feature big casts that are beyond the budget of all

2   BC has the highest rates of unvaccinated kids in Canada. Because "believe the science ... unless it contradicts my stupid, dangerous beliefs."

but the large regional companies. It's amazing what you can do when you don't pay actors. This category includes the Cleland Community Theatre in Penticton, the Powerhouse Theatre in Vernon, the Peninsula Players in Sidney, and Langham Court Theatre in Victoria. I once saw a terrific amateur production of *Cabaret* at the Centennial Theatre in North Vancouver starring, and this is absolutely true, Neil Diamond tribute artist Bobby Bruce. So there is a wide range in the quality of shows available, although not often the actors, many of whom will have all the range of a Crossman BB gun.

Most common audience reaction in the lineup at the concession during interval: "I've seen worse."

In New York, audiences for Broadway shows who are considered unsophisticated are called "the bridge and tunnel crowd." In Toronto's professional theatre scene, they are referred to as "905'ers," in Victoria "Langfordians," in Vancouver the acronym "SOHNOR" or "South of Hastings, North of Richmond" is used, and in Richmond the disparaging term for pretentious theatre goers is "Vancouverites." Kamloops, needless to say, does not differentiate between sophisticated and unsophisticated audiences. No one in Kamloops qualifies as "sophisticated." Having said all that, the biggest problem with theatre is they strike the sets but not the actors.

Comedy Stuff

If you enjoy a good laugh and aren't up to date on the latest idiocy perpetrated by local government, BC is home to one of the best stand-up comedy scenes in Canada. You can catch a show at the inevitable Yuk Yuks in Vancouver and Abbotsford, Lafflines in New Westminster, the Giggle Dam in Port Coquitlam, or Hecklers in Victoria, which has to be the most inappropriate name for a comedy club since Big Al

Hittler's House of Mirth No Relation shut its doors. You can find touring acts and local comics in almost any bar or tavern that has noticed comedians will work cheap.[3] A word of warning: A lot of open mikes and amateur nights will feature young men talking about their genitals. Or, as this is known in the world of comedy, "celebrating their shortcomings." But have you tried the wings?

Unlike other provinces in Canada, such as Alberta, Saskatchewan, Manitoba, Ontario, Quebec, New Brunswick, Nova Scotia, Prince Edward Island, and Newfoundland, the sketch comedy scene in British Columbia (and Labrador) is virtually nonexistent and the quality of improv comedy is mediocre at best. Other than Victoria's renowned Sin City, the live improvised serial featuring the finest troupe of improvisers in the country creating an unscripted weekly show. The exception that proves the rule.

Paintings and Stuff

If you're interested in viewing internationally renowned art from internationally renowned artists, go to the Bill Reid Art Gallery in Vancouver, the Robert Bateman Centre in Victoria, or, if you're looking for works by Toni Onley, Oak Bay's Winchester Gallery or the Lloyd Gallery in Penticton. I always admired Onley's minimalistic renderings of BC's islands and oceans and considered him an impressionist—until I moved here and had the surprising revelation that he was just painting what he saw. You can also find First Nations art in galleries across the province and in most gift shops. Check the bottom before purchasing. That soapstone sculpture may have come from Singapore, not Salmon Arm. And

---

3   I am deliberately not going to mention the Kamloops Komedy festival held in mid-August. First of all, because I don't want any comedian friends to end up stranded in Kamloops; and second, because the festival is just one more inappropriate "K" away from an unfortunate acronym. The producer is Leland Klassen, so it may already be too late.

look for totem poles. They aren't just works of art; they are part of the history of British Columbia.

You can also find totem poles in museums. Vancouver has the Museum of Vancouver, Nanaimo has the Nanaimo Museum, White Rock has the White Rock Museum ... You may, once again, be noticing a pattern. Victoria's museum is called the Royal BC Museum, just to change things up and, I'm assuming, to make sure their anti-monarchist mayor doesn't set foot in it.

If you prefer the sort of art that gets painted on the side of a building, and here I'm talking about murals rather than graffiti, you can find some excellent examples of this type of public art in most towns and cities in the province. If you're looking for graffiti, just stand still long enough in the neighbourhoods of Gastown, Fernwood, James Bay, and College Heights (or anywhere in Kamloops) long enough and somebody will tag you. If you're in Victoria, stop by the main branch of the public library. There's a parking lot across the street that features the worst mural in all of Canada.[4] Vancouver has an annual Mural Festival, and the town of Chemainus features so many murals you should really stop and take a picture in front of the only building that hasn't been painted. It's like my biggest claim to fame: I'm one of only three Canadians who haven't taken a selfie with our current prime minister.

Writer Stuff

If you're a fan of the written word, here's some good news: British Columbia is home to many authors, writers, poets, playwrights, and even the odd cartoonist. Cartoonists are usually very odd. In Vancouver, you could bump into Douglas

---

4   My brother Will goes into detail regarding this *objet d'art* in his Leacock Award–winning *Beauty Tips from Moose Jaw*. He was just visiting. I have to live with this monstrosity. Every time I go pick up a book.

Coupland, Jane Munro, John MacLachlan Gray, or, if you end up at an off-leash dog park, Kevin Chong. Just don't ask him about Neil Young; he'll talk your ear off. If you're in Victoria, Leacock Award–winning author Mark Leiren-Young can be found hugging whales and saving trees,[5] and if you go grocery shopping, you could run into Esi Edugyan at the local Thrifty's. If she's shopping with her husband, Steven Price, you get a two-for-one deal on literary encounters: he's an award-winning poet and she's a two-time Giller Prize winner. Salt Spring Island is home to so many authors your chances of running into somebody who hasn't been published are slim. It's kind of like the murals in Chemainus. This also applies to Sooke. Gabriola Island is where Edd Uluschak, the world's best editorial cartoonist, keeps his drafting table; Alix Hawley makes her home in Kelowna; mystery writer James Osborne hails from Vernon; and Jack Knox has somehow managed to overcome the disadvantages of being born and raised in Kamloops to become a best-selling humourist and the finest newspaper columnist in Canada. I will note, however, that he now lives in Victoria.

If you go into any library in any town anywhere in the province of British Columbia you will encounter a display of books by local authors. Unlike the rest of Canada, this doesn't mean books by writers who live in the province; it means books by folks who actually reside in that specific town. That's how many writers live here. Why, you ask? Here's the deal. If you originally hail from, say, North Bay, Ontario, or Selkirk, Manitoba, or Climax, Saskatchewan,[6] and you end up making a living sitting at a computer writing words that you later press "Send" on ... Well, it will occur to you, sooner or later, that you could be doing the exact same

---

5   Or is it the other way around?
6   This is the real name of a real town. Just down the highway from Big Beaver.

work someplace else. The weather in Victoria is challenging, but not as challenging as in the rest of Real Canada, where winter holds an icy grip for much of the year, only to be replaced by "our bugs are the size of flying hamsters" season, also called "summer."

Be careful if you decide to attend any literary event that uses the word "poetry." You might think an evening of poets reading from their latest work will be a pleasant way to while away some time and enjoy a cup of fair-trade coffee or ethically baked scones, but it is entirely possible that a spoken word event will break out. Spoken word poetry isn't poetry. I'm not sure what it is, but it seems to consist of people talking really ... really ... really slowly and very, very quietly before suddenly SHOUTING OUT LOUD. It's like abrupt-volume-change stand-up comedy, but without the dick jokes. Or any jokes at all.

Reading Stuff

With the sheer numbers of writers in British Columbia, it will come as no surprise to you that there are also a ton (or "tonne" in metric) of bookstores in the province.[7] I can't walk by any place that sells books without going inside. And once I'm inside the store, I can't seem to leave until I've bought something. Usually a book. Not always. Sometimes a newspaper or a magazine. Mostly reading material of some kind.[8] This is either one of my greatest weaknesses or one of my finest virtues. Either way, I've learned to live with it. Here is a list of some, but not all, of my favourite bookstores, in order of how long it takes me to get to them.

114

7   My turn to quote Margaret Atwood. When she was asked how one might go about becoming a writer, she replied: "Read, read, read, write, write, write." Solid advice from Peggy.
8   If I'm in a Chapters and/or Indigo and I don't care for any of Heather's picks, I'll probably buy a greeting card or some stationery. Or those little tinned mints they keep by the checkout.

1) **Misty River Books** in Terrace. This takes me 16 or 17 hours on the road. It really depends on how much coffee I drink and how many stops I have to make along the way. It's well worth the trip. I find the staff picks are always eclectic and informative, especially Cheryl's.

2) **Books and Company.** I can drive to the Prince George location in 12 hours; it takes me a mere 10 hours to get to the store in Quesnel. In addition to selling books, they also have a dedicated arts space and a dedicated staff. Except for Trevor.

3) **Mosaic Books** in Kelowna is a 6-hour drive or a 1-hour flight. I never fly there because I'm concerned my flight might be diverted and I'll end up in Kamloops. It's safer to go by car.

4) **Talewind Books** in Sechelt is less than 6 hours away, but it's a complicated trip involving at least two, sometimes three, ferry rides to get there.[9] I always stop in Gibsons on the way to take a photo with the Persephone. And eat a burger at Molly's Reach.

5) **Black Bond Books** operate a number of stores under a couple of different names in Vancouver. This is a trip I take on a regular basis. It takes me 3 hours and a bit by car and ferry-boat. Unless the Massey Tunnel is backed up, then it becomes an endless example of the relativity of time. I usually stop in at their Book Warehouse store on Broadway because my nephew Genki Ferguson works there.[10]

6) **Mulberry Bush Book Store** is a couple of hours by car to either the Parksville or Qualicum Beach locations. I occasionally take one of the last remaining buses that still offer routes in BC. Allows me to look at the scenery and not worry about driving.

---

9 I've limited my store visits to coincide with the Sunshine Coast Festival of the Written Arts.
10 As this book was being edited, he sold his first novel, *Satellite Love*. Proud beyond words.

7) Tanner's Books in Sidney is only a 30-minute drive from my house. By bus it takes an hour or an hour and a half, depending on the time of day. I could walk there in about 5 hours, which, considering Sidney is chock full of bookstores, might actually be a thing to do some time in the not-too-distant future. Maybe.

8) Bolen Books is located in the Hillside Mall in Victoria. I have driven there. It takes me about 15 minutes. It takes me about 45 minutes to walk there, which is, weirdly, the same amount of time it takes to go by transit. If only city council wasn't so distracted trying to outlaw poinsettias, they might be able to do something to improve public transportation.

9) Munro's Books is right downtown in Victoria. I have no idea how long it would take me to drive there or how much time I might spend on a bus, articulated or non-articulated, but I can stroll[11] there in 15 minutes. Or longer, depending on how many dogs I stop to pet.

BC is also home to two dozen Chapters, Indigos, Chapters/Indigo, and Coles locations. And there are numerous children's bookshops (Kidsbooks and Dickens in Vancouver, The Children's Bookshop in Sidney, Ivy's Books in Oak Bay, etc.), specialty bookstores dealing in mystery books (Chronicles of Crime in Victoria), scary books (The Haunted Bookshop in Sidney), books about the military and history (the Military and History Bookshop in Sidney), and bookstores that sound like they should specialize in something (Pulpfiction Books in Vancouver, Laughing Oyster Bookshop in Courtenay, Hemingway's Books in Abbotsford), not to mention all the fantastic second-hand bookstores like Kingfisher Books in

---

11   Notice I didn't say "walk."

Creston, or Well Read Books in Nanaimo, or Victoria's Russell Books, which used to operate out of three different buildings on three different levels right next door to each other. They've now consolidated operations under one roof and moved across the street. You could write a book about the Best Bookstores in British Columbia. Maybe somebody has. I'll take a look the next time I'm browsing for something to read. So, tomorrow.

Hollywood North Stuff

It all began with *The Beachcombers*. Filmed in Gibsons, set in Gibsons, it featured Bruno Gerussi as Nick Adonis, Pat John as Jesse Jim, Jackson Davies as RCMP Constable John Constable, Robert Clothier as Relic, and Rae Brown as the proprietor of Molly's Reach. Most episodes centred around Relic trying to steal logs from Nick and Jesse before being foiled. Then everybody ended up at Molly's Reach for pie and olive oil soup. The show launched on the CBC in 1972 and came to an end in 1990. That's not a typo: 18 seasons and 387 episodes, back when the film and television industry of BC filmed shows that were actually set in BC. Then American producer Steven J. Cannell discovered our scenery and low exchange rate and brought *21 Jump Street* north of the border, making a star of pillowy-lipped dreamboat Johnny Depp playing the role of undercover LAPD cop Tom Hanson and also making a star of the pillowy mountains of Vancouver, which played Los Angeles, a slightly bigger stretch as far as casting goes.

There had been occasional film and television projects shot in BC previously. *Five Easy Pieces* had Vancouver Island doubling for Oregon and Washington State way back in 1970, and the following year Robert Altman filmed *McCabe & Mrs. Miller* in Squamish and West Vancouver. The success of *21 Jump Street* and the ability of BC to provide locations, crew, and supporting cast members brought a few more shows up from California. Then, in 1995, the NDP government decided a tax break for film and television would be a good thing to introduce. The idea was that incentives for Hollywood productions would speed development of the local film and television industry. It didn't quite work out as intended. The tax credits certainly helped bring foreign films and television shows to British Columbia, but it turned our local film and television industry into a branch plant for the Americans.

In 2018, more US television series were shot in Vancouver than in Hollywood. And that's not counting feature films, mini-series, or whatever those Hallmark thingies are supposed to be called.[12] In Hollywood, these productions are referred to, bitterly, as "runaway productions." In British Columbia, they are called "service productions," which derives from the habit Canadian casts and crews have of leaping to attention, saluting, and shouting "At your service" to US producers.

Service productions, or "British Columbia's Film & Television Industry" to use the preferred term, employ over 60,000 British Columbians and brought in almost 4 billion dollars (we're talking Canadian dollars, of course, but still...) last year. It's a big industry, renewable, and, mostly, nonpolluting. A property used as a location for a Steven Seagal movie? You never get that odour to go away.

British Columbians are proud of BC's film and television industry and will, if asked, go on at great length about how many shows are filmed here. The industry may employ an awful lot of locals, even if a lot of the productions they work on are awful, but it sure ain't a local industry. It would be nice

12 MOW. Not what you do to your lawn in February. It means Movie of the Week.

if we had a few more shows that were actually set in the same place they're being filmed. You know, like *The Beachcombers*. That would really be something to be proud of. I'm pitching a gritty reboot. When Relic starts giving Nick and Jesse a hard time, they drown him. Then he comes back as a zombie. Who fights crime and stuff.

Other Stuff

If you want to hear well-fed singers belting out larger-than-life tunes in Italian about being a starving artist, there are only two choices available in the province. Fortunately both of these choices are very good. Vancouver Opera is the largest opera company in Western Canada. This does not mean it employs the largest opera singers. Shame on you for thinking that. Pacific Opera Victoria is located, of course, in the provincial capital. So is Ballet Victoria. Ballet BC is in Vancouver. You will have noticed that the same people who named utility companies, Crown corporations, and government transportation departments were also in charge of naming arts organizations. Vancouver Symphony. Victoria Symphony. Surrey Symphony. Kamloops Symphony. Wait, what? Dammit.

Also in the "named just a bit too obviously" category is the Vancouver Puppet Theatre. If you're a fan of anthropomorphic pieces of felt, you'll be thrilled to learn British Columbia is home to some of the best puppet companies in the world, including Vancouver's Mind of a Snail, which specializes in shadow puppets, and Puppets for Peace, which combines puppetry with protesting—a very British Columbian approach. Master puppeteer Tim Gosley makes his home in Victoria as does his Pacific Northwest Puppet Festival. Vancouver's Boca del Lupo is more of a theatre company, I guess, but every show of theirs I've seen has featured

119

actors hanging by safety ropes off a bridge or dangling from a tree, so human puppets.

This category also includes:

Rock and/or roll and/or retirement

Bryan Adams. Barney Bentall. Michael Bublé. Nelly Furtado. Carly Rae Jepson. All famous musicians who originate from British Columbia. Or, to quote David Foster, "BC is the best place in the world to be from." It's also a good place to be retired to. There is a long list of singers, songwriters, singer/songwriters, rock stars, folk singers, and, of course, protest singers who live in British Columbia. Nickelback's Chad Kroeger and spouse Avril Lavigne have "let's live in Malibu" money but make their home on Marine Drive in Vancouver. Diana Krall and her hubbie, Elvis Something-or-other, have "let's live in Manhattan" money but also keep a place in her hometown of Nanaimo. Folk singer Bob Bossin lives on Gabriola Island, just down the road from Marg Sutton. Salt Spring Island has rockers Randy Bachman of BTO and Guess Who fame, Bill Henderson of the band Chilliwack, (and I imagine originally the town of the same name), singer/songwriter Raffi who managed the difficult transition from children's entertainer to protest singer,[13] Tom Hooper from The Grapes of Wrath ... The list goes on and on. Any open mike at a pub in Salt Spring has the potential to look like an induction ceremony in the Canadian Music Hall of Fame. And then there's Joe Keithley, former lead singer for the punk band DOA, now a city councillor in his hometown of Burnaby. Still kicking ass and taking names.

---

13 Not all that difficult if you live in BC; a little trickier anywhere else in the world.

9   Finding a Place to Live

SURVIVING RESIDENTIALLY

There's more to British Columbia than just the Lower Mainland. Not much more, but still. As I mentioned in Chapter Seven, half the population of the province lives in the Greater Vancouver Area. If you can call it living. They crowd together in leaky condominiums, cluster around the only working washing machine in the basement laundry room of walk-up apartments, jam themselves into minuscule micro lofts and diminutive laneway housing, and congregate in postage stamp–sized yards in townhouse complexes. Some people even live in single family homes, also called detached houses, as in "detached from reality." Those people are called millionaires. Unless the single family home they live in is a Vancouver Special. That's called a misnomer. What you need to understand is that the Metro Vancouver area is dense. Also, a lot of people live there.

The cost of housing in the Metro Vancouver area is quite high, if "quite high" is a euphemism for "the most expensive city in the country."[1] If you combined every type of housing that sold last year and then added up the total amount of

---

1   You'd have to be quite high if you thought the rates were reasonable.

money spent buying property last year and then divided that amount by the number of properties ... Lemme see, carry the four, drop the nine ... The average, or mean, price per unit of housing sold would come to, aha, $1,156,050. Yikes. That's not just mean, it's downright nasty.

Following the dictates of Keynesian economic theory, ridiculously high housing costs in Vancouver sent interested buyers further afield into neighbouring communities like Burnaby and Richmond. When the influx of new buyers in those cities caused house prices to spike it was on to North Vancouver and Coquitlam. And so on and so forth. It even affected Kamloops. But it all started in Vancouver. Why, you might ask? Money laundering as it turns out. Wealthy pluto-crats in mainland China viewed Vancouver as a safe place to park their dough, real estate being the preferred choice, to the tune of several billions of dollars each and every year for the past decade, coinciding with the steep annual increases in the price of housing. A remarkable coincidence if nothing else.

What I'm trying to tell you is, even if you're the sort of person who can afford to drop a fistful of Lauriers (in metric: 20 dollars) on a humour book, unless you come from a very wealthy overseas family who are worried about the whimsi-cal nature of your local Communist dictatorship, you won't be able to buy yourself a place to live. So you should rent.

The average rent for a one-bedroom apartment is $2,100 per month. Vancouver prides itself on being above average. In most places, two grand a month would be a mortgage. In the Lower Mainland, that's only a mortgage if you're paying bi-weekly like on the lease for a new Corolla.

The only mildly cheaper option available is to try to get an apartment in a co-op building. Don't do this. If own-ing a condo is the worst possible combination of owning a home and renting a home, living in a co-op is the worst possible combination of living in a condo and living with your parents. Condo board meetings are usually dull, and are governed by the Strata Property Act, the legislation enacted by the province of British Columbia to provide standard regulations and procedures. Co-op board meetings are more like attending a Harv Eker seminar or being sentenced to a re-education camp. Oh, they're still dull but you really have to pay attention. They are governed strictly by hurt feelings and collectivism, you know, like a maladjusted family or a wildly ineffectual cult.

If, however, money is less of a concern for you than, I dunno, quality of life or lifestyle or whatever, or maybe you're not planning to stick around British Columbia long enough to contemplate declaring personal bankruptcy, then what you need is a little information on the different and varied communities you may want to spend some time in. I'm happy to help out and pleased to put together yet another list, this time in alphabetical order:

1) **Abbotsford**—*population 141,397.* The largest, most ethnically and culturally diverse municipality outside of Metro Vancouver. Abbotsfordians are happy to be located just far enough away to avoid hockey riots.

2) **Armstrong**—*population 4,815.* This is where Armstrong cheese used to come from. The local company was purchased by Dairyworld, then sold to Saputo and shut down after 100 years in operation. Hard cheese.

123

3) **Burnaby**—*population 232,755.* BC's third-biggest city is home to an endless number of high-rises and most of the soundstages and film and television studios in the province. Basically Burbank without the theme parks.

4) Chilliwack—*population 77,936*. Named after one of Canada's classic rock bands, Chilliwack,[2] or The 'Wack, as it's known in some circles, is now considering a new moniker. The choice has come down to continuing with a nostalgia theme and calling themselves Glass Tiger or switching to the more contemporary Nickelback, or "The 'Back." A plebiscite is scheduled shortly, so if you're planning a Lonesome Mary pilgrimage, better make it quick.

5) Coquitlam—*population 139,284*. The sixth-largest city by population is better known as "the gateway to Port Coquitlam."

6) Cranbrook—*population 19,319*. Cranbrookians are proud as punch that professional wrestler Craig Renney, better known by his stage name, Juggernaut, is a local. Also some hockey player named Steve Yzerman.

7) Dawson Creek—*population 11,583*. Not to be confused with Dawson City, Yukon, the Dawson Creek, BC, gold rush began when the show "Dawson's Creek" first aired and tourists challenged by both geography and punctuation starting showing up hoping to get a glimpse of teen heartthrob Joshua Jackson.[3]

8) Delta—*population 99,863*. Delta is actually three different communities; you got your North Delta, your Ladner, and your enigmatic and unpronounceable Tsawwassen, home to the ferry terminal and the largest outlet mall in the province.

124

9) Greenwood—*population 708*. The Prince Edward Island of BC communities, this is the smallest city in the province. The average price of a single family detached home in BC's largest

2   The mythic sea serpent Seelkee hangs out in the nearby swampy areas. It has been described as looking like "a two-headed snake," so if it actually exists, it's obviously some sort of prehistoric politician.
3   Actually Canadian. In the "Keanu Reeves is a Canadian" sense.

city? A kajillion million dollars. Average price in Greenwood? Five hundred bucks or best offer. And they'll throw in the propane barbecue.

10) Hope—*population 6,181.* The optimistically named Hope is extremely, even excessively, proud of the fact that the town scenes in the appropriately named action picture *First Blood* were filmed there. This was in 1982. If you stay in Hope overnight or even make a quick stop to gas up and grab a bite to eat, somebody will point out that Sylvester Stallone once famously strolled across the Kawkawa Lake bridge, which the town later renamed the Rambo Bridge in his honour—before it was demolished. The bridge was torn down over a decade ago. Sigh. Any attempt to change the topic will be hopeless. For your own security, the moment *First Blood* is mentioned you should abandon Hope.

11) Kamloops—*population 85,678.* A dystopian nightmare where dreams go to die, the guilty are rewarded, and the innocent are punished. I assume. I've only just driven through but I've heard bad things.

12) Kelowna—*population 117,312.* The seventh-largest city in BC, located uncomfortably close to Kamloops. Fortunately the town of Vernon stands in the middle as a demarcation line between the forces of light and darkness, much in the way Red Deer, Alberta, comes between Calgary and Edmonton.

13) Langford—*population 29,228.* Home of big box stores, chain restaurants, and some of the most affordable housing in the CRD, which ain't saying that much. It's like being the best hockey player in the South Sudan.

14) Merritt—*population 6,998.* The antithesis of the meritless community of Kamloops, home to the Rockin' River Country Music Fest and the Bass Coast Music Festival, the best place in BC to listen to music, drink beer, get sunburned, and possibly develop life-threatening melanoma.

15) Nanaimo—*population 83,810*. This is where the Nanaimo bar originated. Also where charmingly eccentric former mayor Frank Ney dreamed up the Bathtub Race, a regatta where caution, but not personal hygiene, is quite literally thrown to the winds. For a truly authentic British Columbia dining experience, you should eat a Nanaimo bar in a bar in Nanaimo.

16) New Westminster—*population 65,976*. Also known as "New West," but never "newest," almost picked to be the Provincial Capital, a history about which New Westminsterites feel equal parts resentment and relief. Perry Mason and Ironside, both played by Raymond Burr, come from New Westminster.

17) North Vancouver—*population 83,395*. This is where Grouse Mountain is located, home of the Grouse Grind, which is not a brand of ethically sourced, locally brewed coffee but a 2.9-kilometre mostly vertical hiking trail. It's actually the world's longest staircase: 2,830 steps. You'd think they would have installed an escalator by now. Look, I get tired driving 2.9 kilometres, so I can't offer you any insight into the Grouse Grind other than it's probably hard to do. Especially in flip-flops.

18) Oak Bay—*population 18,094*. Oak Bay is one of the last surviving outposts of the British Empire and remnants thereof, including signs refusing service to "Ne'er-do-wells and Welshmen." Once you step Behind the Tweed Curtain you enter a tidy oceanfront community that aspires to be more English than the English and is occasionally mistaken for a historical theme park along the lines of Barkerville. As in any good tourist destination, candy stores or "Sweet Shoppes" abound, as do tea rooms or "Ye Olde Tea Shoppe," and you can wash down a Scotch egg with a room-temperature draught beer (in Canadian: "a cold one") at one of the local pubs or "Pubbes."

19) Port Coquitlam—*population 55,958*. Also known as PoCo, although not associated with or named after the country rock band, Port Coquitlam is where the residents of Coquitlam go to look at buildings built earlier than 1987.

20) Port Moody—*population 32,975*. Bordered by Coquitlam to the east and Burnaby to the west, Port Moody has the cheapest rents in the Tri-Cities area. You'll meet a lot of artistic types there for exactly that reason.

21) Prince George—*population 71,974*. The oldest son of Prince William and his wife, Kate, the Duchess of Cambridge, is the eventual heir to the British throne and future king of England. He is going to be steamed when he's old enough to realize just what sort of town his parents named him after. It could be worse. He could be Prince Kamloops.

22) Revelstoke—*population 7,139*. With white-water rafting, rock climbing, the Revelstoke Canyon Dam, and an adorably small ski resort that features some very challenging skiing, this is the place to go for activities and outdoor adventure any time of the year. If you were expecting me to say something mean, sorry. I've always had a good time in Revelstoke. I usually admire the feat of engineering that is the dam for a couple of hours and spend the rest of my trip watching people rock climbing, white-water rafting, and skiing. It's exhausting and exhilarating.

23) Richmond—*population 193,309*. Also known as 列治文, the fourth-largest city in British Columbia is a terrific place

127

to experience Asian culture, food, and shopping, and may actually be part of Hong Kong. Not really sure. Also where the Vancouver International Airport is located, because every now and then the folks in charge of naming things get one wrong.

24) Sidney—*population 11,672.* Located conveniently close to the Swartz Bay ferry terminal and inconveniently close to the Victoria International Airport, Sidney, also known as Sidney by the Sea, also known as "Canada's only book town" due to the quality and quantity of bookstores, is the only place in BC where you can avoid taking a BC Ferry if you want to go somewhere by sea. The Washington State ferry system picks up passengers in Sidney heading to the San Juan Islands. Sidney is also where old people go to visit their parents.

25) Surrey—*population 517,887.* The second-largest city in British Columbia is home to the Peace Arch Border crossing, where the lineups to get into the United States are almost as long as the ferry lineups in Tsawwassen. For a truly authentic British Columbia dining experience, you should have some curry in a hurry in Surrey.

26) Vancouver—*population 631,486.* BC's largest city is stunningly beautiful at first, until you spend enough time there to realize how crazy the place is. Vancouver is the passive-aggressive supermodel of cities.

27) Victoria—*population 80,017.* The capital city of British Columbia aspires to be carefree and car-free. You can ride a double-decker bus and talk to a two-faced politician, of either the municipal or provincial category. You can attend high tea at the Empress or just get high in front of the Empress from the second-hand smoke. They keep pulling down statues, but if you go to the Inner Harbour, you can see living statues as well as jugglers, magicians, contortionists, and buskers of all kinds, including a guy who dresses up like Darth Vader and plays the violin. The reviews are mixed. If the place starts to get on your nerves, remember that Victoria is a small city surrounded by 12 other small cities. They haven't closed the border. Yet. You can always flee to whichever Saanich is the closest.

28) West Vancouver—*population 42,473.* Not known for night life of any kind, but instead known for old money, oceanfront mansions, and one of the wealthiest postal codes in the province. There are almost as many "Vancouvers" in BC as there are "Saaniches." East Vancouver is not a separate municipality like North and West, it's a neighbourhood of Vancouver and also where a West Van kid goes to get back their bicycle.

29) Whistler—*population 11,854.* The co-host of the 2010 Winter Olympics (theme song: "Here Comes the Rain Again"), Whistler is actually a ski resort with a town attached to it. May actually be part of Australia. Not really sure.

30) White Rock—*population 19,952.* Not a dangerous city to live in, but a dangerous city to leave. Make one wrong turn and you're at the US border trying to explain you aren't trying to cross without a passport, you were just going shopping at Costco. And that bag of legal weed in your glove compartment ain't gonna go over at all with the Border Patrol.

31) Williams Lake—*population 10,832.* Ah, Williams Lake, where the houses have wheels and the pickup trucks are up on blocks. Where the town drunk is an elected position, the food bank got robbed at gunpoint, and hygiene is solely how you greet a pal named Gene. These were the types of jokes I was going to make at the expense of Williams Lake, but then

I read Mark Leiren-Young's *Never Shoot a Stampede Queen*, his memoir of being a young crime reporter for the *Williams Lake Tribune*, and I thought, "Huh, what if they read this book and rather than, y'know, threatening legal action, they, well, beat me up?" Then I thought, "Who reads books in Williams Lake?"

Let's move on to accommodations of a more temporary nature. You may not be looking for a place to live. You may just be looking for a place to stay.

Here's a bit of advice: Hotels cost more than motels. You might want to underline that or use a highlighter pen.

There are hotels and motels unique to British Columbia. Prestige Hotel and Resorts offers fairly high-end rooms and suites at fourteen locations from Smithers to Salmon Arm. Accent Inns is a local chain of motels with five locations across BC. They also offer the more budget-friendly Hotel Zed, a very hip retro brand aimed at younger travellers, in Victoria and Kelowna. And there are a number of independently owned boutique hotels, like the Vernon Lodge;[4] Abigail's Hotel in Victoria; Blue Horizon in Vancouver; the Harrison Hot Springs Resort and Spa, located near the hot springs in Harrison, so another name bereft of allegory; the Oak Bay Beach Hotel, located in Oak Bay near the beach, natch; the Sidney Pier Hotel and Spa, located in Sidney near the pier; and the Nitka Lake Lodge in Whistler, which is, surprisingly, nowhere near a lake.

Here's another bit of advice: Boutique hotels cost more than regular hotels.

Also worthy of underlining and/or highlighting: An Airbnb costs way less than a traditional B&B. The downside?

130

4 Guess where this is located? Go ahead, guess.

You won't get breakfast. The upside? You won't have to talk to your cheerful host at breakfast. Just remember that British Columbia isn't all that keen on the new sharing economy, though, so many municipalities are passing bylaws that force Airbnb operators to register and get licensed, which you should look for when you go online. Then you should book with the unlicensed listings. You'll save more money.

If you're young enough, you may want to stay in a backpacker's inn or youth hostel, available in every city and town in the province, except Oak Bay and West Vancouver, which are youth hostile. You'll make friends, you probably won't get bedbugs, and some of the places you'll stay in will be in spectacular locations. Just remember that a youth hostel is not luxury accommodations, although it beats an SRO.[5]

You can also camp. You can do this in provincial and regional parks. They won't have much in the way of facilities, but they will have the best scenery. That's if you can get in. Most of the parks take advance reservations, and you should book way ahead of time, especially if you're visiting during a long weekend. In keeping with British Columbia's inspired efforts when it comes to naming things, the August long weekend is called, wait for it, BC Day.

If you like the idea of sleeping outdoors under the stars but weren't able to make a reservation in time or are unable to afford the park user fees, you can camp for free in most city parks as long as you pack up and are on your way first thing in the morning. The Supreme Court of BC has been tough on bylaws prohibiting people sleeping overnight on city property. You will be camping with people who probably don't have any choice in the matter, as well as dreadlocked white kids from Quebec backpacking around the West Coast *passant du bon*

131

5   This stands for Single Room Occupancy, a fancy way of saying "slum."

temps aux dépens des contribuables de la Colombie-Britannique, so keep that in mind.

I wasn't able to name every single community in this chapter. If you end up in one of the towns I did mention and feel that maybe I was being unfair and even mean-spirited for the sake of a cheap laugh, well, you're right. I'm going to point out that I've been to every one of the towns and cities I've made fun of above. Well, obviously not Kamloops. I want this survival guide to be informative, but not at the expense of my own survival, eh? And if you end up in some place I haven't mentioned, get in touch and I'll try to think of something snarky to say about it.

10 Working Hard and Hardly Working

SURVIVING YOUR EMPLOYMENT

You may only be here for a short time. Or a good time. I'm not one to judge. You could be a tourist or a traveller, soon to be moving on to your next adventure. Thanks for stopping by. You may have come here to be a student and are planning to spend your summers back home with your family. That won't last. You may have moved here permanently to start your new life. It doesn't matter what brought you here. What does matter is your ability to purchase transactional goods and services. You will have to buy stuff in order to survive. You're going to have to pay for food and shelter. You might want to pick up some clothes or souvenirs, maybe pay a cover charge at a comedy club. And you know what? They ain't giving that BC Bud away for free.

One of the first things you'll notice is how expensive it is to live here. BC stands for British Columbia, but it also means "big cost" and "bring cash."[1] If you drive, you'll notice it costs a lot to fill up. The province has the most expensive gasoline in the country. We're number one! We're number one! Why so costly, you might ask? Well, taxes mainly. When you pay at the pump you also pay a provincial motor fuel tax of 7.75 cents

---

1 Or you'll end up with "bad credit."

per litre. This doesn't sound so bad, except you also pay the provincial carbon tax of 8.89 cents per litre, something called the BC Transportation Finance Authority tax which comes to 6.75 per litre, and, if you live in Vancouver, a municipal motor fuel tax of 1.75 cents per litre as well as—yikes—18.5 cents per litre that supposedly goes toward paying off all those SkyTrain stations. Victoria, not to be outdone, adds a municipal transit tax of 5.5 cents per litre on anybody with the temerity to gas up within city limits. Then you got your federal tax of 10 cents per litre and the Goods and Services Tax, or GST, of 5% that is applied to the total cost, including all the taxes. Between 2018 and 2019, fuel prices rose 32 cents per litre. And it ain't getting cheaper.

So, with provincial taxes, federal taxes, super-duper extra-special municipal taxes, and a tax on top of the taxes, almost 50 cents of every litre of gasoline sold in Victoria goes toward taxes. In Vancouver, every litre of gas has 60 cents of taxes on it. Nice racket. Now, you might not drive. Don't own yourself a car, didn't rent a car, and you might think the cost of gas doesn't really affect you. Well, it does. When gas is expensive it raises the cost of every form of transportation—ferry rides, taxi rides, airplane rides, even public transit—that relies on it, as well as the cost of getting all goods to market, as Milton Friedman's monetarist economic theory would put it. So food gets more expensive, travel gets more expensive, food that has to travel gets more expensive, and it all trickles down to you, the consumer.

If you're picking up groceries you will have noticed that British Columbia is one of the few places where it really is cheaper to buy local. Those out-of-season strawberries from California flew to the grocery store. Wait until they come in season and pick them up at your local farmer's market for a lot less. Local strawberries also have the advantage of tasting, well, like strawberries. A neo-Malthusian economist would refer to this as "positive market advancement," which is a fancy way of saying "every cloud has a silver lining."

And check out the price of a pack of cigarettes. I guess if the cost of living goes up, the cost of dying should go up along with it. Smokes are so expensive in BC, they're starting to be used as currency, like in prison or during the last days of the Weimar Republic. But nobody likes a quitter.

The point is, a double-double from White Spot is gonna cost you money, especially if you wash it down with a double-double from Tim Hortons. One of the best ways to be able to pay for things, according to Irving Fisher's economic modelling theory, is through materialistic productivity exchange. In other words, you're going to need a job.

The good news is, despite the astronomical taxation and high cost of living, the economy of British Columbia is humming along and the job market is strong. BC has the lowest unemployment rate in the country. There is a possibility that this is because of and not in spite of how expensive the place is. Right now, in the province of British Columbia, reasonably priced housing is available and there are plenty of jobs. Just not in the same locations. I've noticed over the years that when there aren't any jobs, the cost of living is low, and when there are lots of jobs, the cost of living is high. This might be a pattern, but I'm no economic theorist.

So this chapter is designed to help you find a job. Not your dream job, however, unless you dream of getting a job in the minimum wage service industry. If you're a computer programmer or digital animator, I have even more good news: You are in demand and will easily be able to find a good job with full benefits and at least a six-figure salary. The bad news is that the job will probably be in an extensively renovated and restored heritage warehouse in Yaletown and you still won't be able to afford a roof over your head.

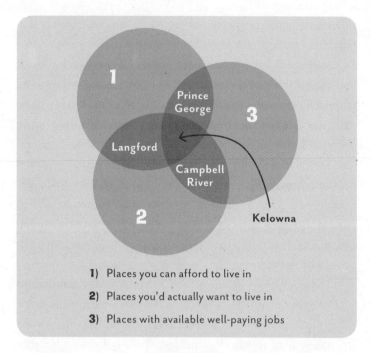

1) Places you can afford to live in
2) Places you'd actually want to live in
3) Places with available well-paying jobs

I have even better news if you happen to be in the trades. A journeyman electrician, carpenter, plumber, pipefitter, welder, bricklayer, carpenter, or mechanic will earn as much as a programmer or digital effects artist. And if you are actually certified, you'll be able to afford to buy a place to live. Also, everybody will be really, really happy to see you. There's a shortage of skilled tradespeople in British Columbia, and you'll make money and make friends, and really, what could be better than that?

Other jobs that are equally in demand, but don't pay quite as well for some reason include nurses, occupational therapists, pharmacists, veterinarians, librarians, and teachers.

However, those jobs are more along the lines of careers, and what you probably want is something that requires a little less commitment but still pays some of the bills. Here's a list of the best entry level jobs, in order of availability:

1) Barista—no surprise here. Every neighbourhood in every community has at least one Starbucks and one independent coffee roastery, often right across the street from each other. If you know your way around a grinder and can keep a straight face when charging $6.39 for a single gluten-free chocolate chip cookie or an organic wild blueberry muffin, this is the job for you. You have to enjoy coffee, of course. If you hate coffee, Tim Hortons is always hiring.

2) Wellness Professional—this job is available if you're in good physical condition. Let me rephrase that. This job is available if you look good. Your actual health is irrelevant. Don't let the term "professional" in the job description concern you; there are absolutely no licensing requirements for being a personal trainer, Zumba dance instructor, or fitness bro. You might get tired of hearing Calvin Harris sing "I Found You" over and over again on heavy rotation, though.

3) Nutrition Advisor—again, no licence, training, or experience is required. Just the ability to gently tell people that maybe, just maybe, they should eat a few more vegetables. Come on, it'll be empowering. You will have the option of working for any number of diet and health clinics, many of which have the name of some doctor in the title. An honorary doctorate still makes you a doctor, apparently. You could also work at the Tim Hortons of weight-loss clinics, Jenny Craig, or even Pennington's. The places aimed at a male clientele all use some variation of "weight management" in their company name because apparently men don't need to lose weight, they need to boss it around.

4) Marijuana Store Clerk—there used to be an abundance of retail positions available selling weed back when "medical" marijuana dispensaries outnumbered Starbucks. Then the federal government decided to legalize pot, which meant

137

rules and regulations and the inevitable bureaucracy, which meant that all of a sudden BC Bud was harder to get hold of than the last gherkin in the pickle jar.[2] Only a handful of legal outlets have opened, and they may not be hiring yet, but if you stand in the parking lot with a case of Hawkins Cheezies and some bags of Dad's Cookies, you'll make enough money and you won't need a job. Or, because legal weed is difficult to purchase, you could go old-school and become a dealer or "BC buddy," which would be an excellent company name if you decide to franchise.

5) Background Performer—another entry-level job that requires no actual training, skill, or even motivation, background performers used to be called "extras" and are still referred to by film crews as "moveable props." There are a lot of shows filming in BC, so demand is high and you won't need professional headshots or a resume. Look up the nearest background casting agency. They'll sign you up faster than a time-share salesman in Vegas. The days are long, monotonous, and completely devoid of glamour, but you'll get a free meal and there's always the possibility you'll be bumped up to SOC[3] and make a little more dough. You will never be promoted to actor. If you can't get that thought out of your head, this isn't the job for you. First and foremost, a background performer needs to know their place. And if the second AD hasn't called you to set, that place is in holding, or what civilians call "a leaky tent."

6) Yoga Instructor—this one takes a little training and a certain amount of flexibility, both physically and morally. You also have to be able to pretend that the system of stretching, balancing, and calisthenics Richard Hittleman introduced

---

2   Helpful hint: Use an olive fork.
3   Silent on Camera, meaning you got to act just a little bit, even though you didn't have to say any words. Some extras like to call this "Special on Camera." Don't believe them. There's nothing special about it.

on television in the 1970s is part of a 5,000-year-old mystic tradition—and not cultural appropriation. It's a bit of a tricky balancing act, but that's what the Half Moon pose is for. If you end up in a studio that teaches "hot" yoga, you should be aware that excessive sweating can make some Lululemon tights see-through and that PVC yoga mats will trap odours. You won't get the images out of your mind or the smell out of your mat.

7) **Telemarketer**—this is a good job if you hate people. The hours are flexible and the money isn't bad, since people tend not to accept minimum wage for jobs that involve having invective and abuse shouted at them for an entire shift. The best companies to work for aren't trying to sell anything to the person on the other end of the phone, they just want their opinions, which become information they can use to sell something to some other person. Statistical analytics and tactical algorithms do most of the heavy lifting. So a market research company like Convergence or Sentis, or a polling outfit like Angus Reid or Ipsos Facto, would provide potentially less verbal abuse and significantly less fluorescent lighting than your typical boiler room operation.

Then there's a long list of jobs you could get that you won't want to do. These jobs will sometimes pay well, but are almost always available because there's a lot of turnover. The reason there's so much turnover is because these are jobs that are downright dirty, demanding, dangerous, disheartening, demoralizing, depressing, or any combination thereof. Listed in order of lower-back pain, these include:

1) **Tree Planter**—demanding, dangerous, and dirty. You'll smell worse than a hot yoga studio at the end of your shift. You might think you're gonna be helping the environment, but what

139

you'll really be doing is hurting your back. If you can maintain the proper attitude, though, you won't get disheartened, demoralized, or depressed. Bit of a cautionary note here: vegetarian food will be hard to come by. You will need to consume two to three times your normal daily caloric intake in order to do your job, and that's hard to achieve eating lentils.

2) Fire Fighter—I'm not talking about the sort of fire fighter who eats firehouse chili in a firehouse with a Dalmatian by their side. Those fire fighters are civil servants who get paid extra for shift differentials and weekend premiums. They also have a pension plan. This type of fire fighter goes out into the forest and fights, well, forest fires, obviously. Dangerous, demanding, and dirty work, and often disheartening, demoralizing, and depressing as well, since most of the forest fires are caused by human stupidity, usually some moron flicking a cigarette butt into the woods.

3) Fast Food Worker—not a dangerous job, usually, but demanding and dirty and demoralizing. You'll have to wear a little paper hat. Your co-workers will be either junior high school students working their first job to earn extra money to buy BTS tickets or senior citizens working their final job to earn extra money to supplement their pensions so they can buy BTO tickets. This is what the fast food industry calls their "minimum wage from cradle to grave" policy, and it's depressing.

4) Fish-Harvester or Fisherman—not the kind who stands with a reel and rod on a bucolic embankment or out on a lake in a metal skiff, but the kind who goes out on a boat with a crew who look like a bunch of pirates and smell like a bunch of pirates who just finished a hot yoga class. Demanding and dangerous and dirty, and, simply because the money is so good, also depressing when a job you took to pay off your student loans turns into your career and all your hopes and ambitions slowly fade away into the ocean mists. Also, you'll never want to eat fish and chips again as long as you live. That's a high price to pay.

5) Writer—not demanding or dangerous, but usually disheartening, demoralizing, depressing, and often an unpaid position. You do get to work in your pajamas, though, so you'd have that going for you.

6) Clerk of the House for the Legislative Assembly of the Province of British Columbia—this is a disheartening, demoralizing, and depressing job, especially if you are a British Columbia taxpayer. For the clerk, it's only dangerous when using the wood splitter and only dirty in the political sense.

Now, those jobs all pay pretty well—even writing, as long as you stick to screenplays and pilot episodes and stay away from poetry and literary fiction—but you're not going to get rich with any of them. If your moral compass is in the repair shop, though, you might be contemplating more of a high-risk-high-reward business. Like a life of crime. If you want to make some serious coin and don't know enough about real estate to launder money, then I suggest you become a con artist or "Howe Street Investment Adviser."

This is where the big money is. Rob a guy of 50 bucks (or a "William Lyon McKenzie King" in the old imperial system of weights and measures) and you'll most likely go to jail. Rob a guy of 50 grand in a swindle and you'll walk away free and clear.

British Columbia has almost nonexistent enforcement regarding white collar crime. The regulatory law is the weakest in the entire country, and the entire country being Canada, it's not like BC is playing against the varsity or anything. It's all penny stocks, shell companies, and sharpies looking for the next mark without fear of any consequences. Beware anybody who calls themselves an entrepreneurial investor or venture capitalist. They won't actually have any capital until they steal from you with a contract.

If money isn't really an issue, then look for some volunteer work. Help out at a seniors' home, or a food bank, or an afterschool program at the nearest church or community centre. Go pat doggies in an animal shelter. That would be fun for you and the dogs. There's a lot of help needed. Despite how prosperous the province of British Columbia is in general terms, there are lots of people who fall through the cracks. You can donate money—or time, which is actually better than giving money. Just remember the old saying: "If you can give, give. If you can't give, don't give. Just don't take."

One final thing: You may have had difficulty following the theories of John Maynard Keynes (who was just trying to figure out how the Great Depression happened), Milton Friedman (who was just trying to figure out how the free market actually worked), or Irving Fisher (who was just trying to figure out how debt deflation occurred) presented in this chapter. Do not allow yourself to give in to feelings of intellectual inadequacy. If you were surprised to see them included in what is, after all, merely a book of humour, that's fine. If you're thinking it might be interesting to look them up online and maybe do some further reading, I just want to be absolutely clear with you regarding all the complicated economic monetarist modelling theorems attributed to them ... I made all that stuff up.

11 Higher Education

SURVIVING YOUR SCHOOLING

So you came to British Columbia to further your education. Good for you. Not a bad idea at all, especially if none of the employment opportunities presented in the previous chapter seemed all that appealing to you. You could attend one of the very good trade schools or technical colleges in the province. You would receive solid practical training that would lead to gainful employment. And more time on the jobsite or in the workplace actually doing stuff as opposed to sitting in a classroom. Here are some examples of places to go where learning leads to earning, ranked according to how quickly you'll be able to pay off your student loans:

1) **Sprott Shaw College**—16 locations in British Columbia, from Abbotsford to Osoyoos right into Vancouver and Victoria. They also offer a dedicated School of Trades campus in Burnaby. Also the most annoying jingle ever.

2) **Pacific Sky Aviation**—offers flight training and certification at their location in North Saanich, which is the most welcoming of all the Saaniches.

3) The Finishing Trades Institute of BC—located in Surrey and offers training, skills upgrading, and apprenticeships. If you misread their name as the Fishing Trades Institute, somebody is going to have that up and running any day now.

4) Riverside College Technical School, Mission—offers introductory training as well as transferrable college credit courses, which will give you the right to say you're a real college egghead.

5) Netcom Vocational Training, Port Coquitlam—offers training in partnership with the International Brotherhood of Electrical Workers local 213. Ask your uncle to hook you up.

6) Western Dog Grooming School—will teach you how to trim your pooch and pamper your puppy in Maple Ridge.

7) Truck Driving School—offered at Cranbrook's College of the Rockies. The now-defunct College on the Rocks offered a course combining Mixology School with driver training. It didn't go well.

8) Metropolitan Bartending School in Vancouver—will teach you how to mix drinks, nod patiently, and smile ruefully at customers. The "how to light a cigarette by snapping your Zippo" course is no longer offered.

9) Kwantlen Polytechnic University—offers Cannabis Career Training, which will come in handy if you want to become a marijuana professional, as opposed to an amateur. The course is only available through their Langley location. The homework is intense.

There's also a profusion of dubious-sounding joints that will train you to be a real estate agent, with offers like "We

150% guarantee you'll pass your BC Real Estate Licence exam on your first and only try or double your tuition refunded no fooling," which is absolutely not going to make anybody think about casinos and money laundering.

Then there are the universities. British Columbia has some of the finest post-secondary institutions of higher learning in all of Canada. Your new path awaits you. Go boldly into the future. All you have to do is apply. And send your transcripts. And qualify, obviously. Get a couple of old teachers to write reference letters. Figure out how and where you're gonna live. Oh, and if you're a student from some other country than Canada, a foreigner or foreign student as it were, come up with an average annual tuition of $20,485. Other than that it's full speed ahead!

Even in university there are courses that are more obvious paths to gainful employment upon graduation than others. These tend to be in the fields of Science, Technology, Engineering, and Mathematics, or STEM. If you don't have the kind of intellectual rigour and self-discipline (and if you go into engineering, you'll also need the ability to hold your booze) required to enter a STEM program, don't worry. You can get an Arts education. It will open your mind, broaden your horizons, and give you something in common to talk about in the break room with your fellow sandwich artists.

Once you've entered a faculty of liberal arts program, you should still be careful. If you spot a course with the word "studies" tacked on at the end—"Identity Studies," "Wokeness Studies," or "Victimhood Studies," say—be wary. Put enough of these courses together and you could be unemployable upon graduation unless you want to work either as an instructor in an associated "discipline" (as always the use of ironic quotation marks is intentional and in this case deliberately provocative) or as an activist. You can be both. The pay isn't great, but there's usually not a lot of heavy lifting.

I've complained previously, perhaps incessantly, about the banality of names used on public institutions in British Columbia. It doesn't get any better with universities, listed here in order of the architectural significance of their campuses:

1) University of British Columbia

Location—Vancouver

Established—1908

Motto—*Tuum est* ("I could use some Tums")

Number of faculty—5,475

Number of students—54,500

Former students who became premier of BC—Mike Harcourt, Glen Clark, Ujjal Dosanjh

Former students who became prime minister of Canada—Joe Clark, John Turner, Kim Campbell, Justin Trudeau

Other notable alumni—actor Evangeline Lily, author Pierre Berton, activist David Suzuki

UBC is the biggest and wealthiest university in the province. The Writing Department was once notable, but now the scandal in the Writing Department is notorious.

2) University of Victoria

Location—Victoria, of course. Sigh.

Established—1903, so older than UBC

Motto—*Multitudo sapientium sanitas orbis* ("We need more smart people because the dumb people are ruining the world")

Number of faculty—914[1]

---

1 The faculty-student ratio does not include all the sessional instructors and teaching assistants who do most of the teaching and grading.

Number of students—22,695

Former students who became premier of BC—None, but George Abbot was a cabinet minister

Former students who became prime minister of Canada—none, although Barbara Hall was mayor of the city-state that is Toronto, so that's pretty close

Other notable alumni—Giller Prize winner Esi Edugyan, author W.P. Kinsella, actor Erin Karpluk

UVic designed the entire campus to look like a traffic circle. It's confusing and soul-deadening, and it only looks good from an aerial view. A small percentage of undergrads drop out in their first year simply because they can't figure out how to get from Cunningham to Clearihue.

3) Simon Fraser University

Location: Burnaby.[2] It's nice that they named a university after a person for a change.

Established: 1965

Motto: *Nous sommes prêts* ("I feel pretty")

Number of faculty: 1,095

Number of students: 34,990

Former students who became premier of British Columbia: Glen Clark, Ujjal Dosanjh

Former students who became Prime Minister of Canada: Margaret Trudeau was married to our 15th prime minister and gave birth to our 23rd, so that's got to count

Other notable alumni—Francisco Aquilini, owner of the Canucks; stand-up comic Ed Hill; Mahamudu Bawumia, the vice-president of Ghana ... Wait, what?

147

---

2   Also Surrey. Well, actually in a mall in Surrey. The SFU Central City Shopping Centre homecoming celebrations are held in the food court.

The rivalry between SFU and UBC is well documented. I don't know why, as they have so much in common: Both campuses are located in the middle of nowhere without anywhere near enough parking or public transit available. Both cities are expensive and unwelcoming. The only real difference is you can't find a student at UBC who applied to SFU first and didn't get in.

4) University of Northern British Columbia

Location—Prince George. Not the royal kid but the town in Northern British Columbia, hence the name.

Established—1990, the same year the *Back to the Future* trilogy concluded

Motto—*En cha huná* ("Salmon again?")

Number of faculty—363

Number of students—4,592

Former students who became premier of British Columbia: none yet, but Shirley Bond was an MLA

Former students who became prime minister of Canada: too early for this to happen, but James Moore was a cabinet minister in the Harper government

Other notable alumni: biathlete Megan Tandy, actor Sonya Salomaa, activist Simon Oleny

You can turn the Village People hit "YMCA" into a rousing school anthem simply by substituting a U for the Y, an N for the M, a B for the C, and a C for the A. You're welcome, UNBC orientation committee.

5) University of the Fraser Valley

Location—the Fraser Valley—where else? The campus locations are Abbotsford, Chilliwack, Mission, and Hope.

Established—1974

Motto—Not just another agricultural college

Number of faculty—710

Number of students—15,176

Former students who became premier of British Columbia—give it time

Former students who became prime minister of Canada—someday

Other notable alumni—Hugh Brody, Canada research chair of Aboriginal Studies, and writer Trevor Carolan, which is cheating because they teach there, they weren't students

UFV once held a semi-academic get-together called The Riverdale Universe about the television show based on Archie Comics. The conference started out as a joke, became surprisingly successful, and ended up being taken quite seriously. An analogy for UFV.

6) Vancouver Island University

Location—it happens to be on Vancouver Island—what were the odds?—although this is a much better name than the University of Nanaimo, which people would think was a trade school specializing in desserts

Established—1969

Motto—Matter here

Number of faculty—1,210

Number of students—16,175

Former students who became premier of British Columbia—none, ever

Former students who became prime minister of Canada—none yet, although Paul Manly just became the second member of the Green Party to be elected to Canada's parliament

Other notable alumni—drummer Pat Steward, composer Andrew Oye, singer Andrea Smith

VIU has their motto written in plain English, but most people aren't aware it's taken from the Welsh *"mater yma"* meaning "nothing really matters," so something got lost in translation. Or there are a lot of Queen fans in Wales.

7) Trinity Western University

Location—Langley
Established—1962
Motto—*Turris fortis deus noster* ("A mighty forest is Our Lord")
Number of faculty—317
Number of students—4,000
Former students who became premier of British Columbia—not quite
Former students who became prime minister of Canada—a half-dozen cabinet ministers, including Deborah Grey, but no PM as of yet
Other notable alumni—author Jonathan Auxier, actor Roger Cross, hockey player Ryan Walter

TWU is a faith-based institution. Its attempts to set up a Christian law school were blocked because students would have to sign a code of conduct that critics claimed went against the Canadian Charter of Human Rights. Apparently inclusivity doesn't include different beliefs any more.

8) Thompson Rivers University

Location—near the Thompson River would be my guess and also in Kamloops
Established—1970
Motto—*Quansem ilep* ("Meet me at the Quonset hut")
Number of faculty—400
Number of students—26,600
Former students who became premier of British Columbia—as if
Former students who became prime minister of Canada—hah!

Unless the Green Party does better than expected and Kyle Routledge takes over when Elizabeth May steps down ... I'm not ruling it out.

Other notable alumni—actor Lorne Cardinal, author Steven Galloway, basketball player Kamar Burke

There's a university in Kamloops. I had no idea. This makes no sense. It can't be TRU.

9) British Columbia Institute of Technology

Location—the main administrative offices are in Burnaby, but BCIT, as it's better known, has six campuses scattered around Metro Vancouver like Panago pizza outlets.

Established—1964

Motto—*Quisque dominus summi* ("Thirty minutes or it's free!")

Number of faculty—2,472

Number of students—48,753 (including part-time and continuing studies)

Former students who became premier of British Columbia—not a one

Former students who became prime minister of Canada—an equally small number

Other notable alumni—bachelorette Jillian Harris, actor Sahar Biniaz, director Stephano Barberis

BCIT does look a lot like a prison from the outside, but on the inside it's a very special tribute to Revenge of the Nerds.

10) Royal Roads University

Location—Victoria

Established—1995

Motto—Life changing (en français: *La vie est moche et puis tu crèves*)

Number of faculty—52

Number of students—1,200

Former students who became premier of British Columbia—none, but Greg Moore did get himself elected mayor of Port Coquitlam. And if John Horgan decides to step down, we could do worse than Mitzi Dean.

Former students who became prime minister of Canada—did I mention Greg Moore? Hey, Jasbir Sandhu got himself elected as an NDP MP.

Other notable alumni—astronaut and David Bowie tribute artist Chris Hadfield; actor Nicole Oliver; Joyce Hilda Banda, former president of Malawi

The big surprise is that Royal Roads only dates back to 1995. Being located inside Hatley Castle, which you've seen in every *X-Man* movie and both *Deadpools*, makes it seem like a much older institution.

Then there are the smaller, although still prestigious institutions and colleges. No premiers or prime ministers have been produced, but there are still lots of famous graduates to take a gander at:[3]

1) Emily Carr University of Art and Design

Location—Vancouver

Established—1925

Motto—Don't touch the monkey

Number of faculty—190

Number of students—1,610

Notable alumni—artist, author, and the guy who coined the term "Generation X" Douglas Coupland; singer and songwriter Neko Case; cartoonist Lynn "For Better or Worse" Johnston

2) Vancouver Institute of Media Arts

Location—Vancouver Where else? Sheesh. The imagination.

Established—1995, originally a school for digital design,

---

3   These are supposed to be listed from the esoteric to the recherché, but my editor suggested that maybe this one list could survive without an explanation of how it's ordered. Also, she didn't think it was funny. So we're not going to mention it.

VanArts incorporated the William Davis Centre for Actors Study in 2008. William B. Davis, of course, was the cigarette-smoking man on the *X-Files*.

Motto—If it isn't in frame, you're to blame

Number of faculty—is varied

Number of students—are hopeful

Notable alumni—actor Aaron Douglas of *Battlestar Galactica*; Andrew Herr from *Letterkenny*; that kid you liked in that thing you saw that time

3) Camosun College

Location—Victoria

Established—1971

Motto—We used to be a Normal School, but there's nothing normal about us now

Number of faculty—413

Number of students—19,000

Notable alumni—news anchor for KTLA in Los Angeles and former CHEK weathergirl Michaela Pereira; fantasy author Danielle Bennett; former member of the Imperial House of Japan Her Royal Highness Princess Ayako of Takamado, who now goes by Ayako Moriya because she married a commoner, but it was true love, I tell ya, true love

4) Langara College

Location—Vancouver

Established—1994

Motto—*Eruditio libertas est* ("Knowledge is freedom," or "If you kill your enemies, they win")

Number of faculty—148

Number of students—21,000

Notable alumni—journalist and national affairs columnist for the *Globe & Mail*, Gary Mason; author Gaurav Sharma; actor Daniel Doheny, who really is that kid you liked in that thing you saw that time

There is also a sub-category, or maybe an actual genre, of post-secondary schools aimed at training you for a career in the film and television industry. Listed here by their proximity to the actual film and television industry:

1) Capilano University—with campuses in North Vancouver, Squamish, and Sechelt, offers a dedicated School of Motion Picture Arts, with diplomas and even degrees being offered in everything from cinematography to costume design.

2) The Gulf Islands Film and Television School—on Galiano Island. Has been offering programs since 1995 to both youth and adult students and was one of the first to offer digital media content creation courses.

3) Vancouver Film School—opened its doors in 1987 and has since turned out wave after wave of skilled screenwriters, camera operators, cinematographers, and directors. Despite the name, they are actually located in the town of Greenwood. I'm kidding. They're in Vancouver.

4) InFocus Film School—also in Vancouver. Offers classes in digital animation and special effects through what they describe as "hands-on" training. It sounds to me like this is where I should go when I need my next batch of unpaid interns.

The film and television industry is always going to need actors, at least until they work the kinks out of AI animation. Universities and colleges offer degree programs in theatre studies, the film schools teach acting, and regular classes are available through most theatre companies. The demand is such, however, that there are also post-secondary institutions that specialize solely in the care and training of actors. If you choose to attend, remember ... it's just a stage.

1) The Canadian College of Performing Arts—located in Oak Bay. Offers a professional "triple-threat" program and has been turning out graduates who can sing, dance, and act since 1998.

2) The Vancouver Academy of Dramatic Arts (VADA)—located in, of all places, Vancouver. Offers an acting program focused on on-camera techniques, and is not to be confused with ...

3) The Victoria Academy of Dramatic Arts—offers a one-year intensive program preparing actors to work in the film and television industry, and is known as VADarts to differentiate it from VADA. They could have just left "Victoria" off the name and called it something more interesting. Island Academy of Dramatic Arts. Next Door to the Mall Academy of Dramatic Arts. Big Joe's House O' Acting. Anything. But, no.

Here's a bit of a warning. Say you wanted to learn to style hair—on humans, not canines—if you attend a reputable school registered with and designated by the Private Training Institutes Branch, or PTIB (pronounced: "perturbed"), the government department that regulates private colleges in British Columbia, your time and money would be well spent.

However, for every type of school listed in this chapter, and for every program I could dream up, from small appliance repair to piano tuning, there will be a private school not affiliated with PTIB that offers way less and charges way more. They don't care if you actually learn English as a

Second Language or if there really is a job market for a Florist Arrangement Technician. They are scams. They are as bad as any Howe Street dump and pumper. They all share the same motto: *Tu autem, homo stultus est argentum cedo*, or "Give us your money, you stupid, stupid people."

12 Having Fun and Making Friends

SURVIVING AND THRIVING

I n British Columbia, if someone tells you to "take a hike," they aren't being rude; they're inviting you to join them in an outdoor activity. One of the reasons human beings ended up at the top of the food chain is that we work together. We're pack animals by nature. It's why solitary confinement is a punishment. If you're in BC for any length of time, you'll want to cultivate more than a garden or weed. You'll want to make some friends. They can help you with the day-to-day eccentricities of British Columbia, and, if things go awry, maybe even help you survive. Try to pick friends who could lift you and carry you for a considerable distance. I'm just thinking worst-case scenario here. By now, hopefully, you've had a chance to look around, which means you've probably noticed that much, if not most, of BC can be lived outdoors. The locals are healthy and active. This can be annoying if you're looking for more sedentary ways to relax and meet people, but if you're reasonably fit, engaging in outdoor pursuits is one of the best ways to meet people, make friends, and have fun. And get in a good workout.

For those of you who consider dripping in sweat and gasping for breath pleasurable, here are some recommendations, along with some slightly less taxing options for those of you who prefer more relaxing pursuits or would prefer to survive while you thrive.

Surviving Climbing and Thriving at Strolling

I mentioned the Grouse Grind, located in North Vancouver, in Chapter Nine. You start your climb on flat ground, or the "North Vancouver Plateau," and ascend 2,830 stairs for a 2.9-kilometre hike (in that other system of weights and measurements: 1.8 miles) that takes you to an elevation of 2,800 feet (in metric: 854 vertical metres, which doesn't sound nearly as impressive), where you can gaze out from the peak of Grouse Mountain and feel a real sense of accomplishment, perhaps even serenity. You'll also feel light-headed. What you won't feel is alone. The Grouse Grind is almost as crowded as Mount Everest. Most people can complete the hike in around two hours; some have been known to run all the way up to the top in forty-five minutes or less. If you try to do this, you will make it halfway up and vomit. The people rushing by you won't be offended, although their looks of sympathy might hurt your feelings. And you'll take the gondola of shame back to ground level.[1]

A slightly less demanding option is to take a stroll around Stanley Park. The park is 405 hectares (or 1,000 acres or 815 kilopascals) large, almost all of it is horizontal, and you can walk the circumference of it in two or three hours without getting tired. Especially if you take a break halfway round for a bite to eat and maybe a cup of tea at the Stanley Park Teahouse (because what other name could they come up with for a teahouse in Stanley Park?) or stop in at the Vancouver Aquarium (sigh) or just park yourself on a bench beside Lost Lagoon, if you can find it, or really anywhere along the way to

---

1   So called because you'll want to avoid making eye contact with the other passengers who made it all the way to the top without throwing up.

enjoy the view. The view will often include Totem Poles, which you should absolutely take a picture of, and racoons, which you should avoid in general. If you try to take their photo, they will ask for payment. And don't feed them! There used to be two types of zoo (the kind that lets you pat the animals and the kind that keeps the animals in a cage) but they've both been closed. People noticed that the animals they were looking at were sad. Almost as sad as human British Columbians. If you've ever tried to pet a depressed goat, well …That ain't a lot of fun. There's still a neat little narrow-gauge train you can ride on, and I urge you to stop at my favourite part of the park, Ferguson Point.[2]

Surviving Swaying and Thriving at Hiking

Also located in North Vancouver, so you might want to make a whole day of it, is the Capilano Suspension Bridge, which was built in 1889 but has been maintained fairly well since then, so you probably shouldn't be too concerned. At 450 feet (in metric: 137 metres) long and 230 feet (or 690 hands) high, it is the third-longest swinging bridge (as opposed to a bridge for swingers) in Canada. The term "suspension" means the bridge is only attached, or "suspended" at either end, and also you should suspend your fear of heights while walking on it. I don't have a fear of heights, but I do have a fear of plummeting to my doom. However, I was still able to make it from one side to the other, albeit weak-kneed and a little shaken. The bridge wasn't shaking or being shaken, thank goodness, but you should be prepared for sudden wind gusts and annoying high school kids, which can both cause the bridge to sway violently. If this happens, you will make it halfway across and vomit. Then you will have to crawl back to the starting point

159

---

2   I'm never sure what I'm supposed to point at. The sunset, I suppose.

on your hands and knees. Again, no one will judge you as long as you managed to miss the bridge deck.

A less queasy choice would be the Sunshine Coast Trail. Or really any one of the dozens and dozens of dedicated hiking trails in British Columbia, from more rugged and rural trails such as the Shoreline Trail in Port Moody that runs alongside Burrard Inlet to more moderate and urban trails like the Galloping Goose Trail that runs from Sooke to Victoria and is also used by bicyclists to commute to work, or even the Othello Tunnels in Coquihalla Provincial Park.[3] These trails have often incorporated former railway trestle bridges, and the view from the top of one of these will easily be as spectacular as from the Capilano Bridge, only they'll be stationary. Unless, you know, the long overdue massive super-thrust earthquake hits, in which case you'll have bigger things to worry about than your acrophobia. I'm only recommending the Sunshine Coast Trail because I completed all 180 kilometres (110 miles or 128 Sheppey Units of Measurement) and am quite proud of myself. The fact that I had wandered away from the Sunshine Coast Festival of the Written Arts and got lost does not make this any less of an achievement.

Surviving Rafting and Thriving at Boating

White-water rafting (soon to be called praecipitium privilege rafting because of a complaint from a Dihydrogen Monoxiderm Studies professor) in Golden is worth the trip and the expense. It will be an exhilarating, inspiring, and inspirational experience. And wet. And pricey. The Upper Canyon section of the Kicking Horse River is classified as a category 3 white-water run, the Middle Canyon is classified as category 4 (or up to 6, depending on how high the water is

---

3   Also a good place to hold a Shakespeare Festival.

and possibly your guide), and the Lower Canyon is a class 5. What does all this mean, you ask? It means that the rapids you will be navigating will range from mildly bumpy to terrifyingly turbulent and the speed you will be approaching them at will range from "speedy" to "aaugh, we're gonna die!" You can book one, two, or all three sections for your trip, depending on how brave and buoyant you're feeling. If you take the full package, they'll feed you a nice grilled steak at the halfway point, but they won't give you any booze until the trip is over. They don't want you to vomit in the raft. Neoprene is waterproof but only stain-resistant. And after finishing the trip, the bright lights and night life of Golden await. I'm kidding, of course. There is no night life in Golden, and even if there were, you won't be interested in going out. You will be bone-tired and you'll just want to soak in a hot bath (or take a hot shower, I'm not one to judge) and collapse into the bed of whichever moderately priced hotel you selected as part of your package.[4]

An equally nautical adventure, with considerably less risk to life and limb, would be to take a BC Ferry trip. Oh, I'm not talking from Departure Bay to Horseshoe Bay or Swartz Bay to Tsawwassen, and I'm not even suggesting you head to Fulford Harbour or Snug Cove. Not that Salt Spring Island or Bowen Island ain't worth a visit, but if you really want to see the wilderness of British Columbia from the water, book a trip on BC Ferries' Route 10, a 274-nautical mile (or 516 kilometres as the crow flies) ride that takes you from Port Hardy to Prince Rupert along the Inside Passage. It usually takes fifteen hours to make the trip one-way, but it can be longer depending on how long they stop at Bella Bella. You will see some stunning scenery and probably meet some interesting folks, but best of

---

4 There are two hotels with reasonable rates. The others are absurdly expensive. You can figure out which is which without my help.

all you'll be able to avoid Triple "O" sauce, because this route doesn't have an onboard White Spot.

Another nautical adventure you could experience without the sort of time commitment (money will be demanded, although usually in a pleasant tone of voice) is whale watching. Orca excursions are offered up and down the coast of British Columbia, with names ranging from the banal BC Whale Tours to the more imaginative Prince of Whales Whale Watching. Cute, eh? If you do get the opportunity to go out on a boat and look at some whales, try to not think about the fact that the Southern Resident Orca population is in danger of going extinct or the fact that your eco-tourism is directly contributing to wiping them out. Make sure you get pictures. In fact, while you're here I encourage you to try to see as much wildlife as you can and take photographs of them before, you know, they're all gone.

If you don't want to wave at whales or go on a long ferry ride, you can still enjoy being out on the water. You can go kayaking and canoeing. This can lead to yakking and canoodling. Just don't go paddle boarding. A paddle board on the water is the equivalent of a Segway on the land. And if you fall in, which you will, the water is cold.[5] You'll get hypothermia. This is a good way to meet people if the people you want to meet are paramedics.

Surviving Sports and Thriving at Culture

If you enjoy paying large sums of money to be surrounded by large crowds of people shouting and complaining (usually about the referee, but sometimes about the cost of a warm watery beer and a cold, unsavoury hot dog), you're in luck. British Columbia has sports teams and sporting events

---

5 You'd know this if you read this book from the beginning.

available all year long. You could attend a BC Lions game at BC Place.[6] BC Place is located in Vancouver, and because Vancouverites aren't as passionate about the Canadian Football League (the CFL motto: 3 downs and a prayer)[7] as, say, Calgarians or Edmontoniates or Saskatchewaners or, as I've already mentioned, most of the rest of British Columbia, tickets will be cheap and plentiful. If you call the box office and ask what time the game starts, they'll ask, "What time can you get here?" The other kind of football is also available. Vancouver's Whitecaps FC play in the MLS or Major League Soccer (what they call football in the USA, which is where the league is located, the film and television industry not being the only branch plants available) and share BC Place with the Lions. BC is also a hotbed for the sport of lacrosse, or "Canada's actual official game, we're not kidding, it isn't actually hockey." Speaking of hockey, Junior A, Junior B, and Major Junior franchises are located in most every city, so you can catch a WHL, BCHL, or VIHL game any day of the week. During winter months only. Curling is available all year. And also, of course, there's the Vancouver Canucks, reportedly a professional hockey team in the NHL, all evidence to the contrary notwithstanding. Their penalty kill may make you want to vomit. There's a minor league baseball team, the redundantly named Vancouver Canadians, that plays out of the eponymously named Nat Bailey Stadium. Who was Nat Bailey, you ask? He was the founder of White Spot. So you can enjoy a double-double and a double play at the same time.

163

For less testosterone-driven group activities, swing by a local pub and catch a local band playing cover tunes and, every

---

6   This is the most boring stadium name in Canada. And that's quite an achievement. Commonwealth Stadium in Edmonton and the Olympic Stadium in Montreal are purely functionary names. Mosaic Stadium in Regina sounds interesting and possibly artistic, but is the result of a sponsorship deal with a potash mining company with the same name, and not, alas, the book store in Kelowna.

7   This would be a great title for a book about the CFL.

once in a while, slipping in some original songs. This activity goes well with beer. British Columbia is home to a surprising number of tribute acts: Vancouver's Blaze of Glory covers Bon Jovi, Burnaby's Abba Again is a Mama Mia tribute band, The Day Trippers offer the inevitable Beatles impersonation, and Gambier Island is home to Bobby Bruce and his Nearly Neil tribute to Neil Diamond. In Victoria, Mike Demers looks and sounds exactly like Roy Orbison and heads up The Lonely tribute, and Syl Thompson channels David Bowie in his A Night of Bowie concerts. If you never got the chance to see the real thing, these are worth checking out, and not ironically. The bands are very good musically and put on great shows.

Now you may be thinking, "Sure, this all sounds like fun, but how will vomiting in public help me meet people and make friends?" Fair enough.[8] Everything I've mentioned so far will offer you the opportunity to interact with other human beings who perhaps share similar tastes in sports or music or adventure. Or walking long distances and being seasick. Whichever. Gotcha. You're probably interested in activities that will allow for more one-on-one interaction. Okay. Let me think. There's always going to a place where you lift heavy objects for brief periods of time and then put them down again, but I don't know much about gyms. You could, I suppose, take a cross-stitch class, which would allow plenty of quiet time to engage in conversation with your fellow needlepointers, or sign up for a square dance or round dance group, but I don't know what the difference between the two would be or even if there is one. You can take free salsa lessons in Robson Square, but I'm not sure if chopping tomatoes, chilies, and cilantro will help you make friends.

So what you might be looking for is advice on where to go to party.

---

8 I did reference regurgitation several times, perhaps excessively. Sickening, really.

In British Columbia, partying and protesting are sort of the same thing. Becoming politically engaged is a faster way to make friends than using online dating apps. Listen for the sound of a drum circle, keep your eyes peeled for placards, follow the drifting scent of marijuana, and you will end up at a protest. You could be at a Save the Whales demonstration one day and a Build the Pipeline march the next. Join in. Chant along. Chain yourself to a tree. You'll be outdoors, unless you get arrested; you'll get plenty of fresh air, unless they break out the tear gas; and you could make the kind of friendships that last a lifetime, unless your friends are undercover CSIS agents, because those guys and gals are notoriously flighty.

The 420 protests used to be a good place to make friends. Every April 20, protestors would show up in great numbers to demand the legalization of marijuana and to celebrate cannabis culture. Drums were drummed, songs were sung, speeches were more or less ignored, and everybody took advantage of the strength in numbers to smoke weed in public en masse. Not just to get high outdoors with a group, but to effect social change. Did you know that marijuana can cure glaucoma? That switching to hemp from paper could save the forests? That marijuana ameliorates the effects of chemotherapy? All true, by the way, and all good reasons to protest and try to change the system.

Then the government of Canada had to go and ruin everything. Not by arresting the 420 dissidents; they'd stopped doing that years ago, unless you were a jerk. Essentially, in BC, if you got charged with possession of marijuana for personal use, you'd ticked off a cop. No, what the federal government did was change the law. They didn't just decriminalize dope, they made it legal. The 420 protests had worked. The pro-marijuana reformers had won. There was no reason to continue. The victory was complete. The 420 protests stopped. I assume. I mean, it's not like the whole 420 thing was really just an excuse to get together, get stoned, and act stupid. Oh, wait, it turns out it totally was: 420 continues unabated, is soon to be a provincial holiday,[9] and is remarkably well organized considering one of things marijuana cures is ambition.

The real secret to having fun and making friends in British Columbia is probably not to spend a ton of time in Vancouver. They're not all that friendly a bunch. That's not to say that you're going to be treated rudely. They just won't really notice you or pay attention to you unless you get in the way. Maybe it's something about having to pay 63% of their monthly income for shelter. Maybe it's the anonymity brought on by the type of shelter they live in. All those shiny glass condo towers contribute to the highest population density in all of Canada. And also the highest number of voyeurs.[10] Could just be simple mathematics. If a certain percentage of the population are self-obsessed and unfriendly, and a whole buncha people are all crowded together like some lab rat behavioural sink experiment, then the odds of bumping into someone who rubs you the wrong way have to go way up. Vancouver was recently rated one of the top ten cities in the entire world to live in according to the EIU's Global Liveability Index, but what do they know?

The city of Vancouver's rather tenuous connection to rock legend Jimi Hendrix is celebrated at the Jimi Hendrix Shrine on Homer Street. The famous "Dude Chilling Park" in Mount Pleasant started as an act of vandalism, then became a joke, and is now the official designated name of a small parkette where dudes can, you know, chill.[11] But there's more to BC than Vancouver. A lot more. There's a wrecked train on

---

9   To be called The Great Canadian Bake-Off.
10 *Naked and Anonymous.* Soon to be a reality show on Discovery Canada.
11 Also dudettes. Chillin' don't discriminate.

Cheakamus Lake Road in Whistler nobody's bothered to clean up. Kinda neat. Or visit Craigdarroch Castle in Victoria. It celebrates the best and worst aspects of capitalism. I'm not going to explain. You'll know what I'm talking about when you go there. Duncan boasts the World's Largest Hockey Stick with attendant puck. The Country Market in Coombs has a roof made of grass and a resident herd of goats to keep it trimmed. There's an entire house made out of recycled bottles near Boswell. They named a stretch of old-growth forest near Port Renfrew Avatar Grove to encourage tourists. It worked.

British Columbia. The last place in Canada the sun sets. The trees are tall, the mountains are snow-capped, the oceans are wide, the sky is endless, the women are intelligent, the men are forthright, and the children erudite.[12]

---

12 Offer not available in Kamloops.

Afterword

You've made it to the end of this book. Congratulations. And you've even decided to read the afterword. Good on you. This is the part of a book most readers skip. An afterword usually talks about how the idea for the book came to be. Now, I'll cover the origins of this book in the acknowledgements,[1] so there's no reason to go on about it here. An afterword can also be a summation of the themes explored in the book. Since the thesis of this book is, quite literally, the same as the title, that seems redundant. Sometimes an afterword is a detailed contextual analysis dealing with the fundamental issues therein. Often it's written by somebody other than the author. Usually for free. We couldn't convince anyone to write the afterword without getting paid, so that's out too.

Really there's no need for an afterword at all. However, when I sent the good folks at Heritage House Publishing the original outline for this book I foolishly promised them one. Sigh. So here we are. Now just in case you think I plan to use this section as a cheap excuse to toss in any witticisms or jokey-jokes that I wasn't able to shoehorn into the rest of

[1] The acknowledgements are another section readers don't bother with unless they work in publishing or are one of the people hoping to be thanked.

the text … relax. That's what *The Survival Guide to British Columbia* Quiz is for.[2]

Now that you've finished this book, let me confess that I'm hoping you did actually purchase it because reading and running at the same time, especially while being pursued, can lead to accidents. You could get hit by a bicycle. There's a reason marathons don't include a written test. The starting line for the Totem to Totem 10K is right by the library, but the Skidegate Band Council would rather you check out a book for before or after the marathon, not during.

If you've picked up *The Survival Guide to British Columbia* in a second-hand bookstore or a remainder bin, my hope is that the information provided within the book is still applicable and relevant. The secret to writing a humour book that has a long shelf life is to not include anything that has a best before date. I told Lisa Helps this very same thing when we had lunch at Pluto's Diner and discussed the planned renovations to the Plaza Hotel. So, if you're reading this book in the future and wondering why I keep pointing out the inadequacies of the Vancouver Canucks penalty kill, it's because I'm gambling the team is still going to, well, suck. If, for some reason, they don't suck, I can only assume all the good teams in the NHL were raptured up when the time-space continuum ruptured during the big galactic expropriation of 2040. But I digress.

Mainly I want to use this afterword to address the good people of Kamloops. Both of them. I kid. There's probably more like a dozen or so good people in Kamloops. However to all Kamloopsinarians who read this book, first of all, I'm sorry

169

---

2   Oh, and the footnotes.

I used so many words. I hope your lips didn't get tired. Second of all, you may feel that I have an unfair opinion regarding your community. You would be correct.

You may wonder why. Is it because I had an unpleasant experience in Kamloops? Not really. I've managed to limit my exposure to a quick deke off the TransCanada to gas up at Super Save before continuing on to more civilized climes. Is it because Kamloops was settled by the Welsh? That's not it, and may not even be factual, although if this is true, it would explain a lot. Could it be the complete lack of anything remotely approaching architectural significance? Don't know. I have no idea what the downtown of Kamloops looks like. Or even if there is a downtown at all, or just an endless array of shopping malls, one after the other, stretching out into the endless horizon.

So why pick on Kamloops? They did remove the cowboy hat and gun from Kami the Fish, also known as Kami the Trout and Kami the Kamloops Trout, but that honestly didn't bother me. How's a fish going to shoot a gun anyway? I was more upset when Prince George picked Fraser the Moose as their mascot. I was rooting for Larry the Unemployed Lumberjack. Apparently he looked too much like a dissolute Mufferaw Joe.

The great playwright and Leacock Award winner Dan Needles, in his capacity as an after-dinner speaker and, until recently, the Honorary Mayor of Mariposa, had an excellent answer when asked how he chose which people to gently chide and which institutions to make fun of. "I pick the people with the broadest shoulders," he said. "I only make fun if I know they can take the joke."

This is a great answer. For anybody Dan Needles picks on. If you have a sense of humour and a sense of self-worth, you can handle some jokes at your expense. So, to all the

Kamloopers whose feelings I may have hurt, let me just compliment you on your broad shoulders, your resilience, and your ability to handle some admittedly cheap shots, and … Hey, you know what? I have a great idea. Here's how you can even the score.

First of all, get in touch with Shane Woodford or Brett Mineer at Radio NL (610 on your AM dial) and get them to whip up whatever passes for a media frenzy in Kamloops. Maybe get *Kamloops This Week* on board too. Then you'll want to arrange some sort of public protest. Now, I'm not suggesting a good old-fashioned book burning, the optics on that sort of thing are bad, and there's a risk of starting a forest fire. What you do is get Kamloops Mobile Shredding Services or Interior Vault on board as a sponsor and have yourselves a new-fangled "Shred *The Survival Guide to British Columbia*" party. You'll be pleased to know that bulk purchases can be arranged directly from Heritage House Publishing. They may even offer a discount. Buy a couple of pallets full of books and shred 'em in the public square. That'll really show me. And we'll all feel a lot better. Heck, you could make it an annual event.

To conclude, I would like to offer up a story that I believe contains all of the glorious contradictions inherent in the province of British Columbia. I was prepping a feature a few years back, and needed temporary production offices. I ended up in a building in downtown Victoria. Not an actual office building, just a building that had offices in it. There's a difference. The main floor had a body shop[3] and a barbershop that catered to servicemen from CFB Esquimalt. The young fellows coming in for a "high and tight" looked just how you'd want members of the Armed Forces to look: Like

171

---

3   Not the Body Shop that sells bath bombs, the kind that fixes dents in cars.

taller versions of Audie Murphy or, for a more contemporary reference, shorter versions of Chris Hemsworth.

The second floor was a rabbit warren of offices. There were a lot of sole-practitioners. Not accountants and law-yers and doctors, but still professionals. There was a bookkeeper, a paralegal, and some sort of therapist who realigned spines. Also a tattooist and an acupunctur-ist, who shared one wing of the building. I don't think they shared needles. Every conceivable age, race, and background was represented in those offices. Everybody seemed to be doing okay, and we all got along. Meaning we nodded at each other in the hallway and otherwise basi-cally ignored each other.

Then a group moved into the empty office next door to mine. They couldn't agree on where the furniture should be placed, or how to set up their reception area, or even what artwork should go where. They argued about every-thing, they yelled, they threw things against the wall, and they slammed doors. They hauled their bicycles up the stairs instead of using the rack provided. They left notes in the kitchen telling us not to place non-vegetarian food in the shared refrigerator. They complained about the appar-ently triggering effect of the military presence downstairs. They were all horrible, horrible people. That group was the Contemplation Society of Greater Victoria and the Gulf Islands.

Now, this sudden change in social dynamics could have caused the rest of us to become equally rude and ill-mannered, even turn on each other like cornered Norwegian wharf rats, but it had the opposite effect. We pulled together with plucky resolve. We started talking to each other. The conversations mainly consisted of "What the hell?" but still. We decided to take action. We were all united: gay, straight, brown, beige, young, old,[4] it didn't matter. We had a common cause. We had meetings. We organized. We held a protest.

It worked. The Contemplation Society packed up their crystals and their aromatherapy candles and buggered off. Peace and quiet returned to the building. And we all went back to ignoring each other. It was the perfect ending.

---

4   The old one would be me.

The Survival Guide to British Columbia QUIZ

You've read the book. You've skipped the afterword. Now take the quiz. It's time to see how much you've learned about A) British Columbia, B) British Columbians, and C) British Columbianisms. This is a multiple choice quiz, just like the tests offered at the finest post-secondary institutions in the province, only with far more intellectual rigour. The quiz is divided into three separate categories: General Knowledge, Notable British Columbians, and Wilderness Survival Tips. The answer key is on page 189.

General Knowledge

Let's see how thoroughly you made your way through the book. If an irate bookseller is still chasing you, throw them a Queen Elizabeth (in metric: 20 bucks) or a couple of Sir John A's (colloquially: a tenner) and find yourself a quiet place to read before attempting any of the questions in this section.

1. BC is an acronym used for British Columbia, but it is also used as an abbreviation that means:

    A) Bring Cash, as it is an expensive place to live, work, or visit

    B) Beyond Canada, because it is isolated from the rest of the country

    C) Banning Cars, Vancouver and Victoria only

2. British Columbia is located:

    A) to the west of Alberta, geographically

    B) to the left of Alberta, politically

    C) underneath Alberta, alphabetically

3. The population of British Columbia is:
   A) almost 5 million
   B) mainly concentrated in the metropolitan Vancouver area
   C) disgruntled

4. The three major regions of British Columbia are:
   A) the Interior, the Coast, and the Lower Mainland
   B) Vancouver Island, the Mainland, and the Gulf Islands
   C) the Good, the Bad, and the Ugly

5. The three major religions of British Columbia are:
   A) Christianity, Hinduism, Sikhism
   B) Judaism, Buddhism, Islam
   C) Hockey, Yoga, Real Estate

6. The weather in British Columbia is:
   A) mild on the coast, cold in the north
   B) mainly wet with occasional sunny breaks
   C) unrelenting

7. Highways in British Columbia are:
   A) euphemistic
   B) nonexistent
   C) bendy

8. BC Ferries:
   A) is a former Crown corporation now operating as a publically held company responsible for providing passenger and vehicle ferry services for the province while somehow also being an extension of the highway system
   B) are the best place to serve fish 'n' chips from White Spot to an orca
   C) are magical creatures often mistaken for hummingbirds

9. The coat of arms of British Columbia:

A) represents the historical ties the province has with the United Kingdom

B) depicts an elk and a bighorn sheep above a setting sun

C) is what you wear to protect yourself from sunburn and mosquito bites

10. The provincial motto is:

A) *Splendor Sine Occasu*: "Splendour without diminishment"

B) *Logica Absque Ludicio:* "Decisions without logic"

C) *Si Vos Fumigant Habere*: "Smoke 'em if you've got 'em"

11. The highest point in British Columbia is:

A) Mount Waddington, 13,186 feet high

B) Fairweather Mountain, 4,663 metres high

C) the nearest 420 rally, where everybody's high

12. The flag of British Columbia consists of a representational Union Jack with a royal crown in the centre, a stylized sun, and three wavy blue lines which represent:

A) why the province is called "British" Columbia

B) the sun setting on the British Empire

C) the effects of climate change on rising sea levels

13. The Golden Goal:

A) was scored by Sidney Crosby in overtime at the 2010 Winter Olympics, giving Canada the gold medal over the USA

B) was scored by Marie-Philip Poulin in overtime at the 2014 Winter Olympics, giving Canada the gold medal over the USA

C) is a Chinese buffet restaurant

14. The 2010 Winter Olympics were held in:

A) Vancouver

B) Vancouver and Whistler

C) pretty much the only part of Canada that can't guarantee snow in February

15. Salmon:

A) are ubiquitous

B) are declining

C) is the first word a British Columbian sings when attempting the Rodgers and Hammerstein standard "Salmon Chanted Evening"

16. BC's biggest exports are:

A) coal

B) lumber

C) environmentalists

17. BC's biggest imports are:

A) oil

B) electronics

C) money

18. Expo 86:

A) was the World's Fair held in British Columbia in 1986

B) created the SkyTrain, BC Place, and Canada Place

C) is the reason you can have a beer on Sunday

19. The Prince of Whales is:

A) a company offering marine wildlife adventures

B) an unpresidential way to refer to the heir apparent to the British throne

C) Aquaman

20. The best thing about British Columbia is:

A) the scenery

B) the people

C) the weather

Notable British Columbians

I've dropped me some names throughout the different sections of this book. A lot of famous people have come from British Columbia, some famous people have moved to British Columbia, and a lot of British Columbians have become famous people. The chances of bumping into a local celebrity are quite good. You could be strolling down Baker Street in Cranbrook, walking up Bernard Avenue in Kelowna, or wandering around any of the Gulf Islands and a prominent British Columbian could cross your path. Speak softly and approach them slowly. They can be timid and easily startled. They won't be wearing a name tag, so you might not know you've met an actual famous person until after the fact.

This section of *The Survival Guide to British Columbia Quiz* is to test you regarding the notable British Columbians you are most likely to run into. Think of this as an abbreviated version of *Who's Who* of British Columbia. For those of you too young to remember, *Who's Who* was how we used to look up famous people before Google. Again, the celebrities you're about to be quizzed on actually hang around BC and you are quite likely to encounter them at a shopping mall or a coffee shop or a protest rally. You'll want to make a good impression, and, as the saying goes, knowledge is power. Let's see how powerful your knowledge is when it comes to the following acclaimed residents of BC:

1. Evan Adams:
   A) is an actor
   B) is a doctor
   C) is no relation to Bryan

2. Pamela Anderson:
   A) is an actor and model
   B) also a passionate advocate for animal rights
   C) is the ultimate Canadian

3. Randy Bachman:
   A) is a rock star who formed The Guess Who
   B) is a rock star who formed Bachman-Turner Overdrive
   C) is a rock star who formed Brave Belt

4. Ed Bain:
   A) has been "The Weather Guy" on CHEK Television since
      1999
   B) has been the host of "The Q Morning Show" on CKKQ
      radio since 1987
   C) is the author of the *87th Precinct Mysteries* since 1956

5. Lorne Cardinal:
   A) is an actor best known for playing the role of Davis
      Quinton on *Corner Gas*
   B) loves rugby almost to the point of obsession
   C) can wear the same clothes that I do

6. William B. Davis:
   A) is an actor famous for playing the cigarette smoking
      man on the *X-Files*
   B) is the founder of the William Davis Centre for Actors Study
   C) is the reason I know that faeries aren't real

7. Gordie Dodd:

  A) is a businessman and philanthropist based on Vancouver Island

  B) is the star of a series of dreadful television commercials that occasionally go viral

  C) with a name like Gordie, he has to be a hockey player, right?

8. David Foster:

  A) is a music producer and songwriter

  B) is the creator of the charitable David Foster Foundation

  C) is the name of an embarrassingly unfinished pedestrian walkway

9. Barbara Todd Hager:

  A) is an award-winning documentary filmmaker

  B) is the author of an acclaimed biography of Shania Twain

  C) isn't returning my phone calls

10. Jack Knox:

  A) is a *Times-Colonist* columnist

  B) has been nominated twice for the Stephen Leacock Medal for Humour

  C) is the brand of gelatin most preferred by Welsh homemakers ·

11. Mark Leiren-Young:

  A) is an award-winning journalist, humourist, playwright, screenwriter, and filmmaker

  B) is a passionate environmentalist

  C) can usually be found at Pagliacci's

12. Elizabeth May:

A) is the leader of the Green Party of Canada

B) is the MP for Saanich-Gulf Islands

C) is the answer to the question "Who will hold the balance of power after the next federal election?"

13. Steve Nash:

A) was an All-Star eight times in the NBA

B) is a future Hall-of-Famer in the NBA

C) is the reason Vancouver no longer has a team in the NBA

14. Ross Rebagliati:

A) is a professional snowboarder

B) is an Olympic Gold Medallist

C) is BC's most famous stoner

15. Mike Reno:

A) is the lead singer of Loverboy

B) is a member of the Canadian Music Hall of Fame

C) is still rocking the headband look

16. Seth Rogen:

A) is an actor

B) is a comedian

C) is BC's most famous stoner

17. David Suzuki:

A) is a scientist and environmentalist

B) is a television personality known for *The Nature of Things*

C) is the guy who lives in that massive house on Point Grey

18. Meg Tilly:

    A) is an Oscar-nominated actor

    B) is a notable novelist

    C) is a brand of hat popular with baby boomers who like to travel

19. Edd Uluschak:

    A) is an award-winning editorial cartoonist

    B) is a three-time winner of the Basil Dean Award for Outstanding Contribution to Journalism

    C) is impossible to spell properly even if you're sober

20. Andrew Weaver:

    A) is the leader of the Green Party of British Columbia

    B) is a scientist and environmentalist

    C) is famous for the songs "Pay Me My Money Down" and "Green Sleeves"

Wilderness Survival Tips

You may have noticed that a lot of the advice in this book applies to the more urban centres. As I've pointed out, that's where most British Columbians live. The population of the province is 4,750,000 give or take, and 2,760,000 or so live in urban centres of the Lower Mainland with an additional 500,000 living in the cities that make up the Okanagan and another 380,000 people who live in the capital regional district. So, uh, that makes the percentage of urbanites versus the total populace, um ... Let's see ... Divide by 12, carry the 9 ... 87%. Whew. People cram together in the cities, with about 5,400 people per square kilometre in the Metro Vancouver area, for example; compare that with 5,400 kilometres per person in the Kootenays. I think. Math is hard.

If you eliminate the populated areas of British Columbia, a tempting proposition, what's left over is still larger than the state of California, which in turn is larger than the United Kingdom. To put it in Canadian terms, the sparsely populated area of BC is greater than the entire province of Saskatchewan or thirty-two Prince Edward Islands. So a lot of the joint is nothin' but geography. If you end up hiking, biking, or camping in one of the empty areas of the province, you're going to need specific survival tips that don't necessarily apply to Aldergrove or Coldstream or Brocklehurst or some other compound-worded neighbourhood.

This section of *The Survival Guide to British Columbia* Quiz will help you survive if you end up in the wilderness and keep you safe if you encounter wildlife.

1. Urban wildlife includes racoons, mice, rats, flying rats (seagulls), crows and/or ravens, red squirrels, grey squirrels, and even the occasional flying squirrel. Which one of the following animals would you only encounter in the wild?

A) The Great Blue Heron

B) The White Tailed Deer

C) The Sunburnt Tree Planter

2. The Great Bear Rainforest is the world's largest coastal temperate rainforest and home to the Kermode bear, also known as the Spirit bear. This bear has white-ish, blonde-ish fur and is:

A) a subspecies of black bear

B) a polar bear that made a wrong turn on the way to Churchill, Manitoba

C) a vain grizzly bear that uses Nice'n Easy

3. Yellow-bellied marmot:

A) is the name of an adorable rodent

B) is a squatter at the Empress Hotel

C) is the most downright insulting thing you can call
   somebody in Fort Steele

4. J-Pod:
   A) is part of the southern resident killer whale population
   B) is part of the transient killer whale population
   C) is a novel by Douglas Coupland

5. In BC, cougars rarely come into contact with humans. If
you wanted to spot one, the best place would be:
   A) the backcountry
   B) Vancouver Island
   C) yoga class

6. The most endangered species in British Columbia are:
   A) Townsend's mole
   B) tiger salamander
   C) Conservatives

7. BC has a thriving population of proudly Canadian:
   A) beavers
   B) Canada geese
   C) immigrants

8. The only mammal found in British Columbia that can
walk on water is:
   A) the Pacific water shrew
   B) the water strider
   C) Steve Nash

9. If you happen to be where the land meets the ocean, walking on the shore or sitting on a dock, the cutest animal you could ever see would be the:

A) sea otter

B) sea lion

C) sea cucumber

10. Predators who swoop down upon their unsuspecting prey without warning include:

A) eagles, both golden and bald

B) owls, both horned and burrowing

C) politicians, both provincial and municipal

11. Higher ground:

A) is where you should head if you're on the coast and a tsunami alert has sounded

B) is where you should absolutely not go if you're in the Interior and a forest fire breaks out

C) is a local chain of organic coffee shops that also sell edibles

12. Most injuries in British Columbia occur:

A) on unmarked trails

B) on mountains

C) at four-way intersections

13. If you go camping, make sure you bring:

A) matches

B) a flashlight

C) a good book

14. What is most likely to help you get found if you get lost in the woods?

A) a compass

B) your cellphone

C) a deck of playing cards

15. To avoid drowning you should follow the advice of:

A) professional backwoods guides

B) experienced park rangers

C) hipsters

16. To protect yourself from bears you should always carry:

A) pepper spray

B) bear bells

C) liquid honey

17. When hiking, do not get between:

A) a mother bear and her cubs

B) a pack of wolves and their carrion

C) a trail runner and the path

18. You cannot go mountain biking without:

A) a mountain

B) a mountain bike

C) a GoPro

19. If you want to avoid people, the most isolated and empty location in British Columbia is:

A) Gwaii Haanas, located 500 km north of Vancouver Island

B) Savary Island, two ferry rides and a water taxi away from civilization

C) Rogers Arena, during the playoffs

20. The best thing about being outdoors in the wilderness of BC is:

    A) the fresh air

    B) sleeping under the stars

    C) pooping in the woods

Now turn to the next page to see how you did.

The Survival Guide to British Columbia QUIZ

Now that you've carefully considered your replies and answered each and every question in *The Survival Guide to British Columbia* Quiz, it's time to see how you did. For the most part a correct answer is worth a single point. Unless it isn't, or there's more than one correct answer, or I lost track of how the scoring system was supposed to be implemented. There may be point deductions for egregiously incorrect answers. Or bonus points awarded capriciously. Remember, all decisions by the author of this book are arbitrary, whimsical, and final.

General Knowledge

1. Acronyms—the answer is A—not just because the province can be pricey, but also because of the many and varied opportunities available if you want to launder your cash.

2. Location—all three answers are correct. Although British Columbians like to think they are above Albertans.

3. Population—the correct answer is C. Also dissatisfied, discontented, and disaffected.

4. Regions—either A or B is correct. C is only acceptable if you're planning to make a joke about Kamloops.

5. Religions—the correct answer is C. No matter their religious beliefs, all British Columbians pray for the Canucks penalty kill to improve, wish to stay limber, and want divine intervention in the housing market.

6. Weather—the correct answer is A, but give yourself a half-point if you picked B or C.

7. Highways—a trick question. The answer is D, all of the above.

8. BC Ferries—the answer is A. Faeries don't actually exist, and as much as killer whales enjoy fish, they prefer their halibut fresh, not breaded and deep-fried.

9. Coat of arms—the correct answer is B. A would get you into an argument with a local and C is the type of bad joke a good editor would have caught in the first draft.

10. Motto—C, but only marijuana.

11. Highest point—Fairweather Mountain at 15,299 feet high is partly in Alaska, so the correct answer is Mount Waddington, at 4,019 metres, which is the highest point completely inside the provincial boundaries. They don't count any mountains BC shares with Alberta because pipelines.

12. Flag—the answer is A. You should never say this to a British Columbian. If the flag does come up in conversation, go with C.

13. Goal—the answer is A. The 2014 Winter Olympics weren't held in British Columbia, but that was still a beauty goal Poulin scored, eh?

14. Olympics—the correct answer could be either A or B, but if you answered C, give yourself 2 points and congratulate yourself for having more common sense than the selection committee of the IOC.

15. Salmon—A or B gets you a point. C is the kind of joke that gets quoted in a snarky review in the *Georgia Straight*.

16. Exports—the answer is A. It turns out that, despite all the protestations and protests, British Columbia contributes just as much to climate change with their coal exports as Alberta does with oil. Who knew?

17. Imports: the correct answer is C. It turns out they weren't kidding around about that money laundering thing. British Columbia has been the laundromat for billions and billions of dollars in illegal and illicit offshore funds. The provincial economy is basically a Ponzi scheme.

18. Expo 86: any answer is correct, although to pass as a true British Columbian, you should also mutter something about the gentrification of False Creek.

19. Prince of Whales: the correct answer is A. If you picked C, not only are you wrong, but I'm going to point out that Namor the Submariner is way, way, way cooler than Aquaman could ever be. Also "marine wildlife adventures" is just a pretty fancy way of saying "whale watching tours." Them must be college boys.

20. The best thing about British Columbia: either A or B is acceptable. If you picked C, you haven't been paying attention. Deduct 5 points.

Notable British Columbians

1. Evan Adams: give yourself 1 point for A, B or C, all of which are correct, and if you happened to know he's from the Tla'amin First Nation, well done—give yourself an extra point and I would really like you to return my copy of *Smoke Signals*.

2. Pamela Anderson: 1 point for A or B; 2 points if you picked C. Pamela Anderson was born July 1, 1967—Canada Day during our centennial—and was discovered at a BC Lions CFL game wearing a Labatt's Blue T-shirt. You don't get much more Canadian than that.

3. Randy Bachman: if you answered A or B you get 1 point. If you answered C, even if you were just guessing, give yourself 5 points and sing along to "Never Comin' Home" with me.

4. Ed Bain: give yourself a point for A or B; no points for C. Although Ed Bain is old, like really, really old, he's not quite old enough to have written the *87th Precinct* novels. That was Ed McBain.

5. Lorne Cardinal: the correct answer is A, although Lorne does love him some rugby. It's more of a fixation than an obsession, though. He used to play for the Edmonton Druids RFC. Also, he once replaced me in a play and was able to wear the same costume. I'd thrown out my back and he was thrown into the production with only four days' notice. He delivered a better performance than I was capable of after three full weeks of rehearsal. Bastard.

6. William B. Davis: 1 point for answering A; 2 points for answering B, because it means you read Chapter Eleven carefully. You get 5 points if you picked C. William Davis is a lifelong skeptic and member of the Committee for Skeptical Inquiry, which makes his gig on *X-Files* either wildly ironic or highly suitable.

7. Gordie Dodd: 1 point for A, 2 points for B, and 5 extra points if you've watched Mr. Dodd say "I won't be undersold" while dressed like Captain Kirk.

8. David Foster: take 1 point for A or B. You get no points for C, but if the opportunity to stroll the parts of the David Foster Walkway that are actually, you know, finished, presents itself, remember that it's only been under construction for seven or eight years. By the standards of the City of Victoria, that's lightning quick compared to other civic projects like the massively over-budget and years-behind-schedule replacement for the world's shortest bridge that finally, barely, just opened.

9. Barbara Todd Hager: A or B are correct and will earn you one point. Barbara Hager formed the Alliance of Aboriginal

193

Media Producers. I'm also a founding member of AAMP, but I somehow forgot to pay this year's dues, so, uh, er ...

10. Jack Knox—once again, A or B gets you one point. If you wrote on the page "the only notable person to ever come out of Kamloops," give yourself 50 bonus points.

11. Mark Leiren-Young—the correct answer is C. Pag's, as it is known locally, is a Victoria institution, as is owner Howie Siegel. Here's a warning: Not unlike eating at a Chinese buffet, you'll be hungry again after your meal. Not in an hour, in about a month. Mark will probably be there. Ask him how he managed to pick up three Stephen Leacock Medals while only winning one. It's a cool story.

12. Elizabeth May—trick question. The actual answer is D, "turned the NDP into the Social Credit Party."

13. Steve Nash—the Vancouver Grizzlies had the opportunity to sign local boy Steve Nash, not once, but twice, and passed. It bears repeating. Vancouver's NBA franchise passed on franchise player Steve Nash. This angered the basketball gods. The team left town. Steve Nash continued to be one of the greats. Oh, and A is correct, because B is conjecture, although he should get into the Hall on the first ballot. Fingers crossed.

14. Ross Rebagliati—A or B are correct. C is obviously hyperbole. Even though Ross Rebagliati runs a cannabis company, he's not BC's most famous stoner. What about Seth Rogen?

15. Mike Reno—once again, any answer is the correct one. Also, that Loverboy tribute act you're enjoying at your local pub? Actually Loverboy.

16. Seth Rogen—the correct answer is B. A is wrong. He's not much of an actor. He was briefly the recorded voice of BC Transit, before they decided they needed someone with more range.

And he's not BC's most famous stoner. That would be Tommy Chong.

17. David Suzuki—A or B are correct answers. C is incomplete. Dr. Suzuki also has homes in Toronto, Ontario, and Port Douglas, Australia. Oh, and a cottage on Quadra Island.

18. Meg Tilly—A is correct and earns you 1 point. B is also correct and earns you 2 points because good for you that you knew—or guessed—that she also writes novels. Start with *Solace Island* if you haven't yet discovered her as an author.

19. Edd Uluschak—A or B gets you a point. C is just a complaint. Edd and I are collaborating on the book *3 Downs & a Prayer: The illustrated history of the CFL*. His drawings will totally compensate for my jokes, so it should be funny.

20. Andrew Weaver—was never actually a member of The Weavers, so A or B.

Wilderness Survival Tips

1. Urban wildlife—the answer is C, not that tree planters don't venture into urban settings, but once they've had a shower and brushed their teeth they emerge from their chrysalis of cleanliness no longer as tree planters but as human beings. Just like butterflies. Herons can be seen in most waterways in the province that happen to be on their migratory path, and urban deer have become such a problem some municipalities are using birth control to keep their numbers down. Not sure how this works, but I assume they make the deer watch an educational video first.

2. Great Bear Rainforest—the answer is A, and if you knew that the Spirit bear is the official mammal of British Columbia, give yourself an extra point.

3. Yellow-bellied marmot—the correct answer is A. The province of British Columbia is home to three different species of marmots. Vancouver Island is where you can spot the appropriately named Vancouver Island marmot, the mountainous regions of the province are home to the wildly promiscuous hoary marmot, and yellow-bellied marmots hang out in south-central BC. They all stick to their own unique habitats, although there is a yellow-bellied marmot named Roger living in the rock garden at Victoria's Empress Hotel. He apparently hitchhiked from the Interior to the Island eleven years ago, enjoyed the weather, and decided to stick around. Fort Steele is a historic tourist town named after legendary Mountie Sam Steele. It's also a good place to watch recent graduates of the Canadian College of Performing Arts pretend to be Cowboys and Saloon Girls and Prospectors and such.

4. J-Pod—you could answer A or C and be correct. J-Pod, along with K-Pod and L-Pod make up the entire population of southern resident Orcas. There are a total of eighty-one of them at last count. That ain't a lot. Endangered? You bet. Also smart. The smartest killer whales of all, because they are able to tell the difference between a tanker from Alberta carrying bitumen and a cruise ship from Alaska carrying tourists.

5. Cougars—the correct answer is B. Out of a population of four thousand province-wide, it's estimated nearly eight hundred cougars reside on Vancouver Island, giving it the highest concentration of cougars in the world. If you answered A, there's a possibility you might see a cougar if you go wandering around in the woods, but remember the question was about the best place to spot them. And C, of course, is yet another joke that should have been cut in the first draft.

6. Endangered species—the answer is B, not that the Townsend's mole is doing much better. The Lily-livered Conservative, to use the full name, is at risk of complete extinction, but nobody outside of the Fraser Valley cares.

7. Proudly Canadian—the right answer is C. Some of the most patriotic Canadians are also the most recent. I'm going to quote my brother Will Ferguson, who wrote "a Canadian is just an immigrant with seniority." No joke here, just credit where credit is due for a profoundly simple statement about Canada.

8. Walks on water—the correct answer is A. The Pacific water shrew has little hairy feet that form air bubbles that enable it to run on top of water for short periods of time. It's sometimes called the Jesus shrew, because, I guess, it looks Hispanic. The water strider is an insect, much like the brain trust that passed on the greatest Canadian basketball player of all time. Two Times. Morons.

9. Cutest animal—cuteness being in the eye of the beholder, any answer but C earns you a point. Sea cucumbers, despite the name, aren't vegetables; they are nature's horrible, horrendous, hideous mistake. Sort of a cross between a giant slug and a length of garden hose, they are—supposedly— edible. Like Prairie oysters, I assume they are only consumed anecdotally.

10. Predators—British Columbia is home to multitudinous birds of prey, so either A or B will earn you a point. Unlike raptors, politicians don't strike suddenly with ferocious speed or deadly precision.

197

11. Higher ground—both A and B are correct answers. You want to get above the water in case of flooding. Fire burns upwards. So head downhill. C is not only incorrect, according to legal review, it may be actionable. Higher Ground sells coffee. They do not sell baked goods containing tetrahydrocannabinol. Yet. But, and here I'm speaking to their board of directors, it's a pretty good idea, what with the name and all. You're welcome.

12. Most injuries—the answer is C, a four-way stop. No drivers know how to use it properly. All drivers will attempt to wave all the other drivers forward. This will result in a long and frustrating delay. Then all the drivers will suddenly lurch forward at the same time. You'd be safer free-climbing Cypress Peak.

13. Camping supplies—camping season in British Columbia coincides with campfire ban season, so the matches won't do you much good. Bring a book. You can read it by flashlight when it gets dark. Give yourself one point for B or C.

14. Lost—the answer is C. Nobody knows how to read a compass anymore, and without a signal you won't be able to use your smart phone to download an app that will lead you to safety. The best thing to do is sit down and start playing a game of solitaire. Somebody will appear from the woods, tap you on the shoulder, and tell you the Jack of diamonds goes on the Queen of clubs. If you forgot to bring cards, just start loudly talking about politics and someone will step out of the trees to argue with you.

15. Drowning—the answer is C, avoid the mainstream.

16. Bears—the answer is C. Pepper spray just makes you a spicier, more delicious treat and the bells just tell the bears "dinner is served." Squirt the honey on your travelling companion and walk briskly away.

17. Hiking—obviously A or B is correct. You are much more likely to encounter C, however. Trail running is a thing in British Columbia. Trail runners believe the great outdoors is best enjoyed by racing through it at breakneck speed. These are the same people who try to set records on the Grouse Grind. And, I imagine, also rush through museums without looking at anything.

18. Biking—the answer is C. If a mountain biker wipes out in the forest and nobody films it, did it really happen?

19. Isolation—Gwaii Haanas is a national park and world heritage site offering some of the best locations for kayaking anywhere in the world. Savary Island doesn't have electricity. Once the NHL regular season comes to an end, both will be more crowded than Rogers Arena.

20. The best thing about being outdoors in the wilderness of BC—A or B if you're a person. C only if you're a bear.

Now it's time to total up your score. Don't forget to include any bonus points earned while completing the quiz. As well as any demerits or deductions.

If you scored 60 points or more: Congratulations. You are prepared for any eventuality. There isn't anything about BC that's going to catch you off guard. Or you cheated. Either way, good job.

If you scored 30 to 59 points: Well done. You're probably more knowledgeable than most British Columbians. And the stuff you don't know won't kill you. Probably.

If you scored less than 30 points: Obviously this book was snatched out of your hand and only the torn pages of the quiz remained in your grasp. You should have paid at point of purchase.

If you couldn't be bothered to do the quiz at all because it was too much effort, or you got distracted or you just couldn't be bothered: My compliments. That's how a true British Columbian handles things. Now head out to the beach or the nearest patio and take it easy. Have some fun. You can always do the quiz tomorrow. Or whenever. Later.

Acknowledgements

First and foremost, a huge thank you to Lara Kordic. She bought me a coffee and we came up with the idea for this book, which would not have happened without her support. I also want to thank Nandini Thaker for her tireless efforts on behalf of this project. Lesley Cameron was the editor and her input and keen sense of humour was much appreciated. Jacqui Thomas came up with the design and did the illustrations, which were better than anything I could have imagined. Marial Shea did a terrific job as proofreader. Martin Gavin put together the index, normally a section nobody pays attention to, but well worth a read in this case. Leslie Kenny did a stellar job on marketing and publicity. Publisher Rodger Touchie has put together an excellent team at Heritage House Publishing; they went above and beyond and were an absolute pleasure to work with.

Index

About the Author

Ian Ferguson won the Stephen Leacock Medal for Humour for his book *Village of the Small Houses*, and is the co-author, with his brother Will Ferguson, of the runaway bestseller *How to Be a Canadian: Even If You Already Are One*, which was shortlisted for the Leacock and won the CBA Libris Award for non-fiction. His equally unhelpful follow-up, *Being Canadian: Your Guide to the Best* Country in the World*, is hot off the presses, as is *Trudeau on Trudeau: The Deep Thoughts of Canada's 23rd Prime Minister*. Ian was a contributing essayist to *Me Funny*, a celebration of Indigenous humour, was selected for inclusion in the *Penguin Anthology of Canadian Humour*, and was profiled in *Second Chapter: The Canadian Writers Photography Project*. His writing has appeared in *Reader's Digest*, *Maclean's*, *The Globe and Mail*, *The National Post*, and *enRoute Magazine*, among others. For the past ten years Ian has worked as a writer and creative director in the film and television industry. He currently resides in a magical city on an exotic island in the Pacific Ocean ... so, Victoria.